We, the founding members of the Royal Fellowship Society, for the betterment of all humankind, hereby dedicate our lives to the pursuit of Science. We promise to freely share, among all members, our wealth and our knowledge. We shall protect this knowledge and prevent any use of it which could lead to the destruction or suffering of people or nature. We agree to fund the development of research estates on Evergreen Isle, which must be kept secret and always remain self-sufficient. In matters of disagreement, we vow to abide by a majority ruling among members of the Society. Signed,

Caroline Andromeda   Galileo Cassini Andromeda

Democritus Dalton   Marie L. Dalton

Emmy Euler   Archim—

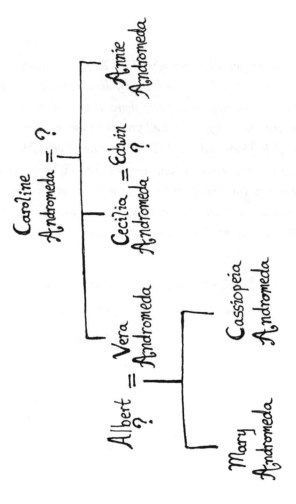

THE ANDROMEDA FAMILY TREE

drawn by Mary Andromeda prior to her adventure on Evergreen Isle

Caroline
Andromeda = ?

Albert = Vera
?   Andromeda

Cecilia = Edwin
Andromeda   ?

Annie
Andromeda

Mary
Andromeda

Cassiopeia
Andromeda

THE JOURNALS OF EVERGREEN ISLE

Book 1

MARY ANDROMEDA

AND THE

AMAZING EYE

J.G. KEMP

For L, C, and D, with love,

– J.G.K.

For teacher guides and contact information,

visit the publisher online at:

storiesinscience.com

"You cannot teach a man anything; you can only help him to find it within himself." – Galileo Galilei

and also, of course...

*...you can only help **her** to find it within **herself**.*

THE DISCOVERY OF EVERGREEN ISLE

From the Journal of Captain Ralph W.

... the sky was ablaze with lightning, and the constant roar of thunder, and wind, and the crashing waves, and the creaking and groaning of the ship filled our ears without pause. Great collapsing walls of water pounded the deck, and the Fellowship Explorer trembled and quaked with the heaving swell, over mountains of ocean and through canyons of liquid sea.

Yet on the night of the third day, the storm weakened, the winds and waves settled, and in the early morning hours, shortly before dawn, the clouds lifted and clear stars shone overhead.

As we gathered on deck and gazed up at the heavens, a faint green and blue glow appeared on the northern horizon —and then pinks and reds and oranges. It was the Northern Lights! The Aurora Borealis! The ribbons of light grew brighter and danced overhead and then a sudden flash pierced the sky—and then another, and another, and another— hundreds upon hundreds of shooting stars! We stood, speechless, transfixed at the scene above, until the wonderful lights faded away into the blue sky of dawn.

And what a dawn it was! On the distant horizon was the storm through which we had passed. By the mighty winds of those terrible clouds our ship had been tossed and tattered, like a child's toy, but we had survived—for days we had survived—and there, there was the rising sun, shining over all.

O sun! Glorious, golden, wonderful light! Our strength was renewed, our spirits refreshed. There was hope! And as we rejoiced in rays of that magnificent orb, a voice rang out—as clear and pure as a bell—and carved deep into my very soul.

"Land Ho!"

My eyes looked to the herald and followed his pointed finger to the west, and there, rising from the sea and cloaked in brilliant green, was the great mountain...

The Island!

CHAPTER 1

THE FORBIDDEN ROOM

Mary Andromeda crept, silently, towards the top of the stairs. She peered between the narrow spindles of the railing, her eyes fixed on the room below, like a lioness stalking her captors from behind the bars of a cage. Her little sister, Cassiopeia Andromeda, followed behind.

"Mary, we shouldn't do this," the younger girl whispered nervously.

Mary's eyes scanned the room—the open entry hall of her uncle's mansion. "Don't worry, it'll just be a minute." She took another silent step forward... and another.

"But... what if we get caught? Uncle Edwin would—"

"He won't be back until after the meeting. We have time." Mary crawled onto the top stair. She listened... she heard the thumping of her heartbeat, and her sister's breathing, and the sound of an airplane outside, and the ticking of the large clock in the room below.

"Mary, I don't—"

"Come on!" Mary pounced down the stairs. Her slender legs blurred under her flapping yellow summer dress, and her curly blond hair bounced with each step. Her sister followed behind.

After reaching the bottom stair, Mary rushed across the entry hall and slipped into a corridor, like a mouse, hunted, running for its life along the cracks of the stone floor. She glanced over her shoulder—no one had seen them—and scurried along, hovering close to the wall, until she reached the end of the passage and stopped in front of a door. An unusually large door. A rose-red door with a strange, spiral letter 'A' carved into the wood. The forbidden door, that she had been told never to open. Ever.

... or so said Uncle Edwin.

Mary withdrew a large metal key, with a similar spiral 'A' design, from her dress pocket.

"Mary, I still don't think—"

"Of course you don't, Cassie," Mary said sharply. "Don't be so afraid." Mary eased the key into the keyhole— metal scraped against metal—the sound echoed down the hallway and throughout the house.

"Shhhh," whispered Cassie.

Mary listened... the house was silent. She turned the key—the lock clicked. "Come on, let's go, hurry." She twisted the knob, flung the door open, brushed her little sister inside, took one last glance down the hallway, and stepped forward, into the Forbidden Room.

Then quietly closing the door behind her, she placed one ear against it, and listened... they were alone. She took a deep breath... and smelled books—musty old books. She turned from the door and gazed at the scene within.

The room was circular, and large, at least two stories high, and there was paper everywhere—piles upon piles of paper—books, journals, and loose pages. Stacks of paper towered above them like the columns of a Greek ruin, and collapsed rows of paper, waist-high, lined the floor like the walls of a maze. Mary imagined huge paper sea-monsters, writhing and thrashing in a rolling paper sea, flinging and hurling paper everywhere, in a violent fury, destroying some ancient and forgotten paper temple.

"What *happened* here?" said Mary, astonished. She stepped towards a collapsed pile of journals which lay near her feet.

"Wow, look at *that*," whispered Cassie, pointing up at the ceiling. It was a sky-blue dome, painted with billowing white clouds, and in the middle was a large circular window, like the pupil of an eye, through which sunlight poured in.

"Why would this room be forbidden?" asked Mary, puzzled. "It's beautiful."

Cassie shrugged. "Maybe Uncle Edwin doesn't want us to see how messy it is?"

"It's just books and journals and paper, what's the big deal?" said Mary. She pushed her glasses farther up her nose.

"*What's the big deal?...* it looks like a library exploded, and then it rained books for a day, and then it all exploded again," said Cassie.

"There has to be *something* here," said Mary, "something more important than messy piles of paper." She picked a journal off the floor in front of her. It was covered in dust. She wiped it off and read the title out loud, "*The Flora and Fauna of Evergreen Isle.*" She thumbed through the pages and stopped at a drawing of a tree and read the caption, "*the Evergreen Isle Cedar is the largest tree species on the island, towering upwards of 30 meters, with a diameter that typically exceeds 2 meters but not more than 3 meters.*"

Mary paused and looked up at Cassie. "Well... that certainly seems like a top-secret, hide-in-a-locked-room, never-let-anyone-read-it sort of thing." She set the journal down and picked up another. "*A Study of Evergreen Isle Tide-pools,*" she read and rolled her eyes. "I better not even open that, sounds dangerous."

Cassie giggled.

Mary liked the sound; she liked making her sister laugh. She picked up another journal, pulled her glasses down to the tip of her nose, stuck her chin up in the air, and read the title in a dignified voice, "*The Mathematics of Evergreen Isle Pinecones.*"

Cassie laughed out loud and then quickly covered her mouth.

"Really? The Mathematics of Pinecones?" Mary said. She picked up another journal, opened it with a flourish, cleared her throat with an aristocratic cough, and read again, *"this unusual pattern of rotation defies the accepted laws of gravity..."*

Cassie laughed harder while trying to muffle the sound with her hands.

"... and is but one of the mysterious," Mary began to gesture with her finger for emphasis, *"... and wonderful ...,"*

Cassie was laughing out loud.

"... qualities of the Andromeda—"

The laughing stopped.   Cassie looked serious. "Andromeda?" she asked, "Who's that one by?"

Mary closed the journal—the cover was blank. She opened it to the first page and read the inscription aloud,

The Journal of Vera Andromeda

"Mom's?" Cassie asked.

"Yeah... I think so," said Mary.

Mary flipped through the journal, scanning the words on one page before turning to another. "Looks like it's about stars and galaxies and gravity, with lots of numbers and charts." She turned back to the first page and stared at her mother's name.

"I like her handwriting," said Cassie.

Mary traced the letters slowly with her finger. "Yeah, me too. Why would Uncle Edwin have Mom's journal in here, and why would it be forbidden?" she asked, puzzled.

"I don't know, but maybe there's more," Cassie said excitedly. She quickly dropped to her knees, pulled a journal from the pile, and glanced inside it... and then set it down and picked up another. Mary joined her.

As the minutes passed, the sunlight pierced through the window overhead, landing on the floor like the beam of a spotlight, and crawled, slowly, over the sea of paper, as the earth turned, and the angle of light changed, and the sisters searched.

"Mary look!" Cassie called out. "Mom's sisters—the ones from the accident." She read, *The Classification and Composition of Stars by Annie and Cecilia Andromeda.*" She flipped through the pages and then frowned and set the journal down. "More stuff about space... nothing about Mom."

Mary picked out an old-looking, tattered journal at the bottom of the pile and opened it. The title was written in flowing cursive script. "Hey! Listen to this!" She read, *The Founding Documents of the Royal Fellowship Society, compiled by Caroline Andromeda.*"

"Grandma?" asked Cassie.

"What's the *Royal Fellowship Society*?" wondered Mary. She flipped through the yellow and brittle pages.

creak...

A sound came from inside the house. Cassie gasped. Mary cocked her ear towards the door. They waited...

BANG—the silence was broken. It was the slam of the front door. They had lingered too long. Uncle Edwin was home.

"Oh no!" said Cassie. She looked at Mary, eyes wide, waiting for instructions.

Mary thought for a moment. "We can't leave now. If he doesn't see us leaving the room, he'll see us leaving the hallway. We have to wait. Maybe he'll go upstairs, or into his office, and we can sneak out then."

A faint sound of footsteps came from the entry hall. Uncle Edwin was pacing, back and forth, at the base of the staircase.

"Oh no, he's pacing again," whispered Cassie, "we could be here for hours."

As they waited, Mary imagined a mouse, trapped in a hole, patiently waiting for the slim chance to slip out, unnoticed, past the dangling claws of a hungry cat. But soon, the sound of the pacing stopped and was followed by the creaking of the staircase and footsteps on the second floor, which gradually moved off into a different part of the mansion.

"Thank goodness," said Cassie, relieved.

Mary listened… the house was silent again. She stood and handed her grandmother's journal to Cassie and smoothed her dress over her legs. "Bring the one from Mom and Mom's sisters. We'll go through the parlor and out the kitchen door to the treehouse. He'll think we were there the whole time. He'll never know."

"What about the key," asked Cassie, "what if he finds it's missing?"

"We'll worry about that later, come on." Mary opened the door as quietly as she could, and Cassie slipped out. Mary followed and then carefully locked the door, dropped the key into her dress pocket, and led the way back down the corridor. *Please don't catch us, please don't catch us,* she thought.

Before crossing the open entry-hall, Mary peered around the corner, up the stairs to the second floor. Uncle Edwin was nowhere in sight. Mary took a deep breath, grabbed her sisters hand, and without saying a word, ran towards the parlor—past the staircase, under the chandelier, and past the front door. *Almost there,* she thought.

She ran through the parlor—past the couches and coffee tables. The kitchen hallway was just around the corner. *Please don't catch us, please don't catch us,* she thought again. As she rounded the corner her foot caught the rug on the parlor floor—she tripped—she tumbled forward. Cassie tumbled into her—the journals fell—the heavy metal key flew out of Mary's pocket. She crashed into an end-table. The key landed, clanking, on the stone floor. The vase on the end-table wobbled, back and forth, before it fell over and shattered next to the tangled sisters...

When the clangor had faded away, the house was silent. Uncle Edwin loomed over them, his arms crossed, his brow furrowed, his black eyes fixed and empty—as usual—like he was staring at something far away. "What's this?" he asked, in his calm, cold, heartless voice, as he slowly reached for the fallen journals and his key to the Forbidden Room.

Chapter 2

Sent Away

The sun was setting, and Mary lay on her bed, staring blankly at a shaft of light which was falling through a crack in the curtains. Specks of dust were dancing, weightless, in the sunbeam, slowly twisting... and spinning... and rolling through the air. Mary imagined she was dust herself, carried up on gentle eddies and floating freely around the room. She heard the chirping of crickets and the hum of an airplane in the world outside. She was hungry; since she had opened the forbidden door, she had been locked in her bedroom, allowed only bread and water, for five days.

The sky grew darker, and the shaft of light slowly faded, and Mary heard footsteps in the hall. She sat upright and straightened her yellow summer dress, and pushed her glasses farther up her nose. The footsteps approached, and a key scraped in the lock. The door opened, and her Uncle Edwin entered.

He stood tall and was wearing his usual gray suit and silver tie. His straight black hair was combed to the side. He was frowning, and he fixed his empty, staring eyes upon Mary. Mary stared back.

"Your mother *left you*, little girl, with *me*," he said scornfully. "*I* decide what you may do, and *I* decide where you will go." He crossed his arms over his chest and stood even taller. "Tomorrow, you will leave this house, and you will go to the Institute. You will stay there... indefinitely. Pack a suitcase, the car will arrive at nine o' clock, do not be late." And he quickly glanced down at his watch and abruptly turned to leave.

Mary was stunned. *Leaving?* "What... what about my sister? What about Cassie?" she said hurriedly.

Her uncle did not stop; he strode out of the room and walked briskly down the hall. "Your sister will remain here," he called over his shoulder.

"What!? No! I won't leave her!" Mary shouted, "You can't—" She scrambled off the bed and began to run after him but Cassie stopped her.

"Mary don't," Cassie whispered, "it'll only make it worse." Cassie had been listening from the hall, just outside the door.

"But—" Mary froze; she couldn't think straight. Cassie's eyes were red and her cheeks were flushed and wet. "But—"

"Please Mary, don't argue with him." Cassie grabbed Mary's hands. "Please."

"But—"

Cassie looked into Mary's eyes, one and then the other, back and forth.

"He can't... I... but..." Mary's words stumbled out. She knew Cassie was right. She knew that arguing with her uncle would only make it worse. She listened to his footsteps fade away in the house and the sound of his office door closing before she retreated, powerlessly, back into her bedroom, back into her burrow. Cassie followed her.

"Mary, what's happening?" Cassie asked fearfully. "What's the Institute?"

Mary pushed the door closed and shuffled to her bed. "It's that *school*, the one in Port Oceanside."

"The one on the island... that you can see from the lighthouse? The one they say is like... a prison?"

Mary settled on the mattress, her shoulders slumped forward, and stared at the rug. "Yeah."

Cassie gasped. "Oh no, Mary—"

"—I'm so sorry Cassie," Mary interrupted. "I should have listened to you. It's all my fault. I never should have taken that key. I never should have opened that door. I should have known better." She clenched her fists and sat up taller. "Now he's sending me away? Separating us? This isn't fair.

Mom said he would take care of us. He can't separate us. He can't. I won't leave you. How can he be so... *ARRRR!*" Mary grabbed a dress off the floor, quickly bundled it into a ball, and threw it across the room. It hit the wall softly and fell, crumpled, like a tissue paper. "*ARRRR!*" she said again, and stood, and picked up a shirt and threw it, and some pants, and two socks, and her pajamas—each hit with a gentle *poof* and landed in a soft pile. When she had thrown all the clothes near her, she slumped down on the bed again.

The wind outside quietly whistled against the bedroom window, and Mary imagined being carried-off on it, carried away, like a leaf, or a feather, or a speck of dust.

"I know," said Cassie excitedly, sitting on the bed beside her sister. "What if we ran away and never came back?" Mary's eyes lit up. "We could hop on a train and ride it to a far-off, exotic, city," Cassie continued.

"Yeah," added Mary, sitting up straighter, "and we could meet handsome princes and live in splendid castles—"

"—and ride magnificent horses with glorious, flowing manes," added Cassie, tossing her curly hair over shoulders.

"Yes, and live as gypsies, playing our violins on the streets for spare change—"

"—and sleep in tents in the forest—"

"—and travel around the whole world—"

"—and..." Cassie paused, her voice became serious, "we could try and find Mom."

Mary was silent.   She looked away and slumped forward again and sighed. "Mom's gone Cassie. She left us. It's better to just forget about her. Trust me."

"But Mary, what about her journal, and Grandma's? There has to be more. Why is Uncle Edwin keeping them in there? He knows everything, he just doesn't want to tell us? Why—"

"—I don't know, Cassie. Please, I don't want to talk about Mom, or Grandma, or—"

"—But Mary, I have to know. I have to know why she left. What if she's still out there? What if we *could* find her? What if—"

"Cassie, stop," Mary said firmly. "We'll never know. It's no use asking. Uncle Edwin is in charge. You're trapped here and he's sending me away and that's all there is to it."

Cassie looked at the floor.   The wind outside was getting stronger. It whistled around the high stone walls of the mansion. It was almost dark. Lightning flashed through the crack in the curtains but there was no thunder; the storm was still far away.

"Mary," Cassie began, "before you have to leave... will you tell me what she was like again... will you tell me what you remember?"

"I've already told you everything I remember," Mary answered flatly.

"I know, but I don't remember anything. Please tell me again. I won't be able to hear it for... who knows how long."

Mary sighed. She didn't want to think about her mother; she just wanted to forget about her.

"Please?" Cassie asked again.

Mary looked into Cassie's eyes. She *couldn't* leave her —she couldn't leave her sister. *Why is this happening to me?* she thought. *Mom promised—* She took a deep breath... and another... and another. "Okay," she finally agreed and pushed her glasses farther up her nose.

"Before we came here, we lived in a small house. I was 5, you were 3. I don't remember much about it, just big mountains and a big tree in the yard that had a swing, and Mom would push me. Her hair was blond like ours, but straight, and she always wore it in a pony tail. I remember one time I fell off the swing and landed on my head, and she washed the blood out of my hair. She had taken her glasses off, and I remember looking up into her blue eyes as she rinsed the soap out and thinking that she was beautiful."

"I remember we were playing in our room one day, when Uncle Edwin came, and he and Mom yelled at each other in the kitchen, about Dad and Aunt Annie and Aunt Cecilia. I remember her crying when she told me they died in an accident, right after you were born. I remember her crying as we drove here. I remember I asked her what was happening, and she said she had to leave, but that we would be safe, and Uncle Edwin would take care of us, and that I should take care of you. And I remember you, crying after her as her car drove away... and that's all, I don't remember anymore."

When Mary finished, Cassie hopped off the bed and began to pace excitedly, like she was thinking hard about something.   "What do you think happened to Dad anyway? Don't you ever wonder... how he died... what the accident was?"

Mary shrugged. "I used to. I don't think about it anymore. What difference does it make anyway? He's gone. Mom's gone."

"Mary—" Cassie's eyes lit up. "While you're at the Institute, I'm going to find out what happened. I'm going to get back in that room. I'm going to find more journals and find out about Mom, and Dad, and Grandma, and the accident. Uncle Edwin can't keep it a secret forever. I promise, Mary. I —"

"No," Mary interrupted, "you can't get caught again. You have to forget it."

"Well, maybe if I get caught again," Cassie argued, "Uncle Edwin will send me to the Institute too, and we can be together?"

"If he wanted to do that, you would be coming already," Mary argued back.

Cassie stopped pacing and thought for a moment and sat back down on the bed. "Yeah—" She shrugged. "I guess you're right."

The wind outside continued to whistle.   More lightning flashed in the distance.

"Mary?" Cassie asked.

"Yeah?"

"Can I sleep in here tonight?"

Mary smiled. "Yeah, I'd like that.   You can help me pack in the morning."

Cassie popped up and hurried out of the room, and Mary walked to the pile of clothes by the wall and pulled out her pajamas and put them on.   In a few minutes, Cassie returned, wearing her pajamas and holding a pillow, and soon, the sisters were lying under the covers, in the dark, staring up at the ceiling.

"Oh Cassie," Mary sighed, "what am I going to do without you?"

Cassie's voice sounded encouraging.   "Maybe the Institute won't be so bad.   You might make new friends... and at least you won't be locked up here."

"Yeah... I'll just be locked up somewhere else," said Mary bitterly.

The wind whistled.

"Remember the dome in that room?" said Cassie. "That was amazing, the way the clouds looked so real."

"Yeah it was," Mary agreed.

"Wouldn't it be great, if your bedroom had a glass ceiling, and you could look up at the stars every night?" Cassie added.

"I guess so," Mary replied.

Lightning flashed through the crack in the curtain.

"Goodnight Mary."

There was a gentle rumble of thunder somewhere far away.

"Goodnight Cassie."

Mary closed her eyes and listened to the sound of her sister breathing, and the whistling wind, and the rumbling thunder; and after what seemed like a long time, she finally fell asleep.

✧ ✧ ✧

It was nine o'clock the next morning. The sky was gray; the air was still; the world looked dull and lifeless.

Mary and Cassie stood by the driveway, at the bottom of the stone stairs that led up to their uncle's mansion. Their uncle, of course, was not there to say goodbye. A black car approached, pulled up next to the girls, and stopped. It was a driverless car—the newest model. Uncle Edwin always had the newest model. The doors and the trunk opened. Mary rolled her luggage to the car and heaved the suitcase into the trunk, and Cassie set a violin case down beside it.

"I don't know if I'll be allowed, but I'll write if I can," Mary said.

"You better," Cassie replied, sniffling.

"Goodbye," said Mary.

"Goodbye," said Cassie, and she wrapped her arms around Mary and sobbed freely.

HONK... HONK... HONK...

The car started honking loudly—it was 9 o'clock. Mary quickly turned away from her sister and crawled into the back seat. The honking stopped, the doors closed, and the car began to drive away.

CHAPTER 3

CAROLINE'S CORNER

The drive to Port Oceanside began on a narrow road that wound up and down and around rolling hills, and past luxurious houses, like her Uncle Edwin's, with their vast green lawns, and white fences, and big stone fountains. The road went through an old forest, where little sunlight touched the ground. The canopy overhead reminded Mary of stained-glass windows. Mary remembered lying on her back, with Cassie beside her, in their treehouse, gazing up through the branches, imagining faces in the leaves and the blue sky beyond.

The trees rushed by, and soon the narrow road became two lanes, and then three lanes, and then four lanes, and the houses got smaller, and smaller, and closer together until there was no space between them at all—no forests, or fields, or hills—just house, after house, after house.

Her uncle's car joined countless others, zooming along, almost noiselessly. Some were driverless, their passengers busily working while they rode, but the rest were driven by people—staring straight ahead, gripping the steering wheels, frowning, like they were in a trance.

Mary had been to the city once before and she hadn't liked it. Everyone had seemed distracted and anxious—they walked quickly and never talked, and their eyes were always fixed on screens in their hands, or in their cars, or on the buildings, or in the restaurants. They were all like her Uncle Edwin, she thought.

The houses rushed by and the car crested a hill and Mary saw the tall buildings and the sprawling city of Port Oceanside. She saw the glimmering blue sea and the Port Oceanside Lighthouse, perched on a hill, overlooking the bay.

Mary had been to the lighthouse, with her sister, on her other trip to the city. It had been turned into a museum, and her uncle had left them there—while he *ran an important errand*—and she and Cassie had climbed, up the winding spiral stairs, to the antique light. She remembered the giant lenses, and the gears, and the motor; she had liked how everything was visible and not hidden away, out of sight. She remembered the observation deck, the view of the city, and the sound of the ocean. She loved the sound of the ocean.

She also remembered Caroline's Corner, a bookshop she and Cassie had discovered nearby; Cassie had to use the bathroom and the one in the lighthouse was out-of-order. Mary remembered opening the door to the bookshop, and a little bell rang. She thought it was so clever and simple, how the moving door made the bell ring, with no wires or batteries or electricity. A woman with curly gray hair and glasses had poked her head out from behind a bookshelf and said, "Oh, hello sweethearts. Let me know if you need anything."

Mary remembered paging through a book, and glancing up, and seeing the old woman had been staring at her, smiling, with kind, loving, caring eyes. Something about the woman had made Mary want to run into her arms and cry, but just then Cassie had come out of the bathroom, and they had to hurry back to the lighthouse to wait for Uncle Edwin.

Mary knew her grandmother's name was Caroline, and since that day, she and Cassie would sometimes pretend that the woman in Caroline's Corner *was* their grandmother. They had never met their grandmother—Uncle Edwin said she had died—but they would play games in which their long-lost Grandma Caroline would rescue them from their uncle's mansion and sweep them away to live happily-ever-after in the bookstore by the lighthouse.

Mary had tried to forget Caroline's Corner, just like she had tried to forget about her mother.

The buildings rushed by, and the car went deeper into the city—towards the ocean, towards the lighthouse, towards the docks and the boat to the Institute. Mary searched for Institute Island in the middle of the bay but could not see it through the haze. She imagined sitting at a desk, all alone, in a small room, behind bars, staring at a screen, without her sister, trapped on an island with no hope of escape.

As the car descended the last steep hill before the ocean, Mary saw the masts of sailboats, and the long wooden docks, and the lighthouse on the hill directly in front of her. The car approached the curb and stopped, and its door and trunk opened automatically.

Mary climbed out. She breathed in the air and the smell of the ocean... she stood up taller and breathed in again... ah, the sound of the water, and the squawking gulls, and a distant horn across the bay! For a moment she forgot everything: her sister, her uncle, the Institute. The smells and sounds of the sea rushed into her. She closed her eyes and breathed deep and the breeze caressed her hair, and her thoughts were carried away on the wind.

HONK HONK it was the car again—two honks, reminding her not to leave without her luggage.

She opened her eyes and saw the lighthouse rising above her, and she smiled and thought of her sister. She glanced at Caroline's Corner—there was a *Closed* sign in the window. She looked towards the docks and saw groups of children and a man wearing a blue uniform. He was pointing at a row of small boats nearby.

Mary lifted her suitcase and violin out of the trunk and stepped onto the curb, and the car drove away. *This is it,* she thought, and sighed, and slowly walked down the dock, towards the crowd, rolling her luggage behind her. As she approached, the attendant in the blue uniform noticed her and spoke:

"Eh, what's your name Miss?" He had shining green eyes and a short white beard and a friendly smile.

"Mary Andromeda," she replied quietly and pushed her glasses farther up her nose.

"Andromeda, eh?" He looked down at the clipboard in his hand. "Right at the top, of course. Last boat, down at the end. Allow me." He reached for her luggage and nodded at the violin case in Mary's hand. "Don't know if you'll need that, not much music at the Institute."

Mary gripped the violin. "Um, can I sit over there," she asked, pointing to a row of benches on one side of the pier, "until it's time to go?"

"Of course, Miss, should only be about..." He checked his watch. "10 minutes. Won't leave without you." He smiled and winked and turned to greet another new arrival.

Mary wheeled her luggage to the benches and sat down and watched the other kids. Many of them seemed to know each other—they were standing together and talking and laughing. *I wonder why they all look happy to go to the Institute,* Mary thought. Some of them wore gray uniforms, while others wore t-shirts and jeans, or summer dresses. *I guess I don't look that different,* Mary glanced down at her own summer dress and smoothed the light yellow, cotton fabric over her legs. As more students arrived, the attendant continued to check his clipboard, point to the boats, and carry luggage on board.

The small boats were driverless, or *captain-less,* Mary supposed. They were enclosed, like a plane, and the stairway which connected them to the dock folded back in, like a door.

When a boat had five passengers, its door would close, revealing the Institute logo—a large letter "I" with a flame on the top as if the "I" were a candle. The boat would then slowly and stealthily back away from the dock, turn towards Institute Island, and shoot out into the bay. Mary wished the boats were open on top, so that she could feel the wind in her hair as she sped across the water.

She watched nine boats leave, one after another, until there was only one left, bobbing gently up and down with the waves. The attendant looked at his watch and then towards the road and then back at his watch again and muttered something under his breath. After a few minutes, Mary heard a car approach.

It was driverless, like her Uncle Edwin's, but even longer, and with tinted windows, like a driverless limousine. A boy stepped out and stood there for a moment, in conversation with whoever was inside, and then the door closed, and the trunk opened, and a robotic arm from inside the trunk pulled out a suitcase and set it down on the sidewalk.

The boy was tall and skinny, with glasses, and dark black hair parted in the middle and combed down. He wore dress-shoes and slacks and a gray collared shirt, buttoned all the way up, with the Institute logo on the front pocket. As he walked briskly towards the dock, the suitcase followed him!

"Mr. Henry Kelvin, sir?" the attendant asked, as the boy approached.

"Yes, yes," snapped the boy, "who else would I be?"

The suitcase, which was still following behind, started making a loud grinding noise. It was stuck, unable to roll itself over a small bump where the planks of wood were uneven. The suitcase backed up, paused, and moved forward, only to be stopped by the same bump. It backed up again, this time turning slightly to the left, and then moved forward, and was stopped a third time. The grinding noise got louder.

The attendant grimaced and reached for the suitcase, but the boy blocked his way. "I've got it!" Henry snapped, and glared at the man. "I don't need *your* help."

The attendant stepped back and tipped his hat. "Sorry sir, my apologies."

The boy struggled with the case, lugging it behind him, and bumped it hard on each step as he descended the stairs to the boat. A few steps from the bottom he let the suitcase go, and it tumbled down and landed with a thud. "Stupid thing!" he muttered.

The attendant shook his head and then faced Mary and smiled. "Time to go, Miss." He took her suitcase and the violin and walked them on to the boat; and as he climbed back up the stairs to the dock, he reached into his blue, buttoned jacket and pulled out a small package. "Oh, almost forget, this is for you," he said and handed the package to Mary.

She took it from him. "What is it?" she asked, puzzled.

"Not sure, the woman in that bookstore asked me to give it to you." He pointed to Caroline's Corner. "Now off you go, Miss."

Mary was stunned. *A package? for me? from Caroline's Corner?* She glanced towards the bookshop—there was no one there. She descended into the boat, her mind racing. *Why would she give me something? How does she know me?* The stairway closed, and the boat began to move. Mary wobbled back and forth and eased herself onto a bench and tore open the package.

It was a journal! A journal exactly like the old, tattered journal she had seen in the Forbidden Room. A journal exactly like the one with her grandmother's name on the cover. She flipped through it... it was blank. She turned to the first page and there, in flowing cursive script, were the words:

> *Mary,*
>
> *It's time you learned the truth.*
>
> *Follow the clues.*
>
> *— Caroline*

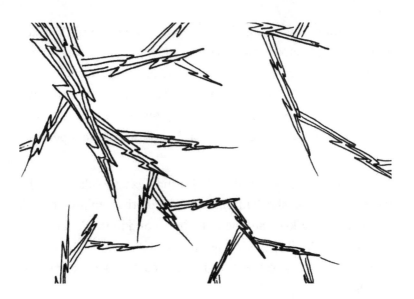

CHAPTER 4

THE UNEXPECTED FLIGHT

"Hey, that's cool," came a boy's voice. "What is it?"

Mary looked up. Benches lined the edges of the boat in a large oval, and the boy was sitting across from her, smiling. He had messy white hair and wore a dark green vest covered in pockets, and he was pointing at the journal in her hands.

The words stumbled out of Mary's mouth. "Umm... it's an empty journal," she mumbled quickly and rewrapped the package on her lap.

"My name's Benjamin... Benjamin Wild... but I go by Ben," the boy said, and he leaned forward with his hand outstretched. "What's your name?" His wide eyes were blue and bright.

"I'm Mary... Mary Andromeda." She shook his hand and quickly let go and pushed her glasses farther up her nose.

"Wow, that's a beautiful name," Ben said excitedly, and then he quickly glanced away. His face started to turn red. "I mean... that's cool."

A girl sitting beside him gave him a gentle punch on the shoulder. "Yeah, it *is* a cool name... *and* beautiful." She winked at Mary. The girl had big, brown eyes and a smile that stretched from ear to ear. "I'm Julee... Julee Joy... and I go by Julee." She elbowed Ben in the ribs and extended her hand to Mary. Her frizzy black hair was braided in two long braids which hung down in front of her shoulders. "I like your dress," she added. "It looks like a sunrise."

"Thanks," Mary replied, "I like yours too. I've never seen anything like it." Julee's dress was a vibrant red and yellow and green, woven with triangle, diamond, and circle designs. Mary imagined the patterns spinning and twisting and blending into each other, as if the dress were alive. "... and your shoes!" Mary added. Julee's brown leather boots were speckled with shiny red sequins that looked like rubies.

"Why, thank you," Julee said in a glamorous voice as she flipped her ponytails over her shoulders. "I know we have to wear uniforms at the Institute. Gray uniforms. Ugh. Who knows how long it'll be before I can wear *these* again." She admired her shoes and tapped them together.

"They're not gray, they're *slate*. There's a *difference*," came another voice; it was the boy who had arrived last, the one with the robotic suitcase. He was staring out the window, eyebrows furrowed, shoulders slumped forward. "... and they're not that bad." He glanced at Julee and scoffed. "Better than ridiculously colorful clothes anyway."

Julee smiled back. "Well, I just hope we don't have to wear... slate... on the weekends." She winked at Mary and then asked the boy. "What's *your* name, by the way?" The tone in her voice was pleasant, like she had a confidence about her, like nothing could upset her. Mary liked it.

"Henry Kelvin. Just leave me alone," the boy answered abruptly and kept staring out the window.

Julee just smiled and shrugged her shoulders.

"I'm Elliot!" blurted a voice. It came from a girl sitting near the luggage rack in the corner. Mary hadn't noticed her. "Elliot Ki. I know it *sounds* like it should be spelled K...E...Y... but it's *actually* spelled K...I..." Elliot reached out and shook Mary's hand.

Elliot looked younger. She had straight black hair, cut to chin-length, and pinned behind her ears with big green hair clips. She wore blue jeans, rolled up to her knees, and brown sandals. Her t-shirt was sea green with pink, tropical flowers printed on it. She reminded Mary of her little sister.

"I had to wear a uniform at my old school," Elliot said, her eyes were wide open, and she was nodding eagerly. "It wasn't so bad. You don't have to worry about what you're going to wear everyday, and no one makes fun of you for being different."

"So, I won't get to wear my awesome vest?" asked Ben excitedly. "Look at all the pockets—some have zippers and some have buttons and this one has another little pocket hidden inside."   He leaned forward, showing-off the secret pocket.   "My mom got it for me, in case we do any fishing at the Institute."

Henry scoffed again from his seat by the window. "You do not go *fishing* at the Institute.   What a suggestion." He looked over Ben's vest and cargo pants and hiking boots. "You don't go *hiking* either."   He glanced at the others and looked back out the window and shook his head.   "New kids," he muttered and rolled his eyes.

Julee whispered something into Ben's ear, and Elliot smiled awkwardly and shrugged her shoulders.   Mary glanced out the window.

The boat began to accelerate, like the others that Mary had watched, and was facing Institute Island which was now barely visible through the hazy air.   The rectangular buildings of the Institute reflected the late morning sunlight like giant mirrors.   Mary felt the package on her lap and her mind started racing again: *it's time I learned the truth—about what? follow what clues? about my mom? the accident? could Caroline—*

"I didn't bring anything to write in," said Elliot, nodding at the package on Mary's lap.   "My dad told me I wouldn't need any paper because everything is on computers at the Institute.   I wanted—"   Elliot suddenly flung forward, out of her seat and onto the floor.   The boat had jerked to the side and had turned towards the open sea.   It was gaining speed.

"Um… what's happening?" asked Julee, nervously.

The boat continued to accelerate. The sound of its engine grew louder and louder and louder, and the boat sped faster and faster and then began to skip, like a stone, bouncing up and down on the water. Mary flew up... and then smacked down on the bench, and then flew up... and then smacked down on the bench.

"Make it stop!" Elliot cried from the floor, her voice barely audible over the roar of the engine.

"Wow, are those wings?" Ben shouted, pointing excitedly out the window.

A sleek white wing, slicing through the water, had extended from the side of the boat. The engine roared louder than ever, and the boat tilted upwards and suddenly, the jolting stopped. The boat was taking-off! It was rising higher and higher into the air!

"I didn't know they could do *that!*" said Henry, with a glimmer in his eyes behind his round glasses.

"What's happening?" cried Elliot, still crouched on the floor. She looked terrified as the boat continued to climb higher. It climbed and climbed and then passed through a thin layer of clouds and then leveled off. The sound of the engine decreased, and, as if nothing was out of the ordinary, the boat cruised along, flying effortlessly, high above the water. Elliot crawled off the floor and sat, confused, back on the bench.

"I've never been on a *plane,*" marveled Julee, gazing out the window at the ocean below.

"Me either," added Ben. "We must be a thousand feet up."

"I was on a plane once... I got sick," said Elliot. She sat with her legs to her chest, hugging her knees. "What's happening, why aren't we going to the Institute?"

"It's simply a computer malfunction," Henry explained casually. He didn't look concerned at all. "They are guided by satellite, I'm sure they will correct the mistake soon."

"Hey, look at that!" Ben pointed towards the front of the plane. They were flying fast towards a dark wall of clouds which suddenly lit-up from a flash of lightning striking within them.

"That doesn't look good," said Julee, nervously. "I hope this thing is safe." She looked around for a seatbelt, but there was none.

"This is an Institute plane," said Henry with confidence. "I'm sure it can handle it."

"But, what if we get struck by lightning?" asked Elliot.

Henry scoffed and explained, "the lightning just travels through the metal of the plane, it can't hurt us."

"Here we go!" shouted Ben as the plane flew into the storm, engulfed by the clouds. The clear blue sky was replaced by darker and darker shades of gray, and the plane began to shake, slowly at first, and then more and more violently. It suddenly dropped in the air... and then recovered... and then dropped again.

"I don't like this," said Elliot; she looked like she was going to be sick. The look reminded Mary of the time Cassie got sick on a merry-go-round, after eating too much. Mary slid next to Elliot and put her arm around her.

The turbulence continued. They were flying incredibly fast, Mary thought, but she wasn't sure, she couldn't compare the plane's motion to anything outside. Through gaps in the clouds, she caught occasional glimpses of the water, far below, and then felt a sinking feeling in her stomach.

"We're losing altitude," declared Henry.

Elliot convulsed like she was about to throw up but nothing came out. A bolt of lightning flashed in front of them, and Julee screamed—"Ahhhhh!"—and the plane dropped suddenly and then tilted forward and began to shake harder than ever. The water was getting closer and closer and closer.

"We're gonna crash!" shouted Ben. "Hold on!"

The nose of the plane pulled up—*smack*—and they touched down on the water. Mary flung forward as the boat skipped across the surface... once... twice... three times. The wings retracted. The roar of the engine died away. Elliot was shaking and gripped onto Mary's arm as the boat moved slower... and slower... and slower.

"Hey, what's that?" said Ben curiously, pointing out the window through the dense fog. Mary followed his outstretched finger and saw, emerging from the mist, the wooden pillars of a dock—ghostly tree trunks speckled with barnacles and slathered in slimy green algae.

"Weird," said Julee as the boat slowly approached the dock and stopped.

A motor whirred, and there was a loud *click*, and the door opened, making a stairway to the wooden planks above. Chill air rushed in, along with the sound of water sloshing and seagulls squawking nearby. Mary shivered as the boat bobbed gently up and down with the waves.

"It's so cold," said Elliot, still huddled on the bench, clutching her legs. "Where are we?"

They all glanced at each other, speechless, as if wondering who would move first. *It's time you learned the truth*, Mary thought. She stood, set the journal on the bench, rubbed her bare arms for warmth, and stepped slowly up the stairs.

The moment she reached the dock, the clouds parted, like curtains opening before a play, and there, through the mist, a colossal mountain towered high above her—snow-capped and the most brilliant green color Mary had ever seen. Out of the corner of her eye she noticed a weathered post and a plank of wood laying beside it. She took two steps towards it and read, carved into the aged wood, in letters worn and barely visible, two words:

Evergreen Isle

CHAPTER 5

THE ARRIVAL

"Wow…!" marveled Ben, who had followed Mary and was gaping up at the mountain. Elliot quickly ran past him, to the edge of the dock; she knelt down, hung her head over the water, and threw up—

"*Bleeeegh….Bleeeegh…*"

Mary crouched next to her and rubbed her back. The dock was cold and wet and covered in bird-droppings, and Mary shivered again.

"I didn't know mountains could get *that* big," said Julee, stepping off the staircase. "Where *are* we?"

"*Bleeeegh….Bleeeegh…*" Elliot threw up again.

"Hey look!" Ben shouted. "A house!" He was pointing towards the shore with one hand, and shielding his eyes with the other.

At the end of the dock, there was a path which wound up to a large white house perched on top of a hill. The hillside glistened from the wet grass, and the house shone brightest of all, as if it was covered in mirrors. The brilliant, white, snow-capped peak towered above. It was so bright Mary had to look away.

"I wonder who lives *there*," said Julee.

Elliot pulled her head back from the edge of the dock and sat crosslegged on the wet planks. "Sorry," she said quietly, and tucked her hair behind her ears. "I get sick easily." She looked down, her shoulders slumped forward.

"Oh, that's okay," said Mary. "My sister gets sick easily too." She stood and held out her hand and helped Elliot stand up.

"It's so cold," shivered Elliot, rubbing her arms.

"I have a jacket in my suitcase," offered Mary, who was cold too, but was starting to feel the warmth of the sun on her arms. Mary glanced towards the boat. Henry was still inside it, crouched over, looking at something in his lap. He noticed Mary watching him and quickly stood up, put the object in his pocket, and climbed the stairs to the dock.

"No, that's okay," said Elliot, glancing at Mary's bare arms. "I think I'll warm up soon."

Henry arrived beside them and frowned at the mountain and the house on the hill. "Does anyone else have a phone?" he asked and looked around impatiently. No one answered. He scoffed, "Well, mine isn't charged. Maybe someone up *there* has one, and we can call my father to get us off this ridiculous island. Whoever is responsible for this... inconvenience... is going to have to answer to *him*. Come on new kids." He rolled his eyes. "What are you standing around for?"

"Um, how do you know it's an island?" asked Elliot, innocently.

Henry scowled at her.

"It is," said Mary. "Look at this." She pointed to the sign that lay flat on the dock.

"Evergreen Isle," read Ben. "I like the sound of that." He gazed up and admired the mountain. "I'm gonna grab my backpack," he added, "be prepared, ya know."

"Hey grab mine too, would ya?" said Julee.

"Yeah, sure thing!" he hollered back as he skipped down the stairs to the boat.

He returned a moment later holding two backpacks. One was tan colored and covered in more pockets than were on his vest. The other was bright red and covered in colorful patches; strings of beads hung down, jangling, all around it.

Ben handed the red backpack to Julee and swung his own over his shoulders. "Come on troop!" he announced and headed off down the dock, like he was on a march. Julee followed behind.

"Um, I guess we're going," said Elliot.

"Yeah, I guess so," Mary shrugged and suddenly remembered the journal—she didn't want to leave it behind. "Hey, wait a second, I'll be right back." She hurried down to the boat. The journal was sitting on the bench, right where she had left it. She pulled her violin case out of the luggage rack, set it on the bench, unzipped a side pocket, slipped the journal inside, and returned to the dock with the case in her hand. Henry looked at her suspiciously before turning briskly and walking away.

"What's that?" Elliot asked.

"It's my violin, I just didn't want to leave it," Mary replied, and began to walk towards the shore with Elliot beside her. "Do you play an instrument?" Mary asked.

"I play piano, but I want to learn the cello. I went to a symphony, with my school last year, and there was a woman who played the cello, and it was the most beautiful sound, the way it echoed through the whole room. I've been asking my parents for one, and they keep saying *maybe*, but then they said I was going to the Institute, and I don't think they have music there." She paused and then asked, "What grade are you in? I'm only 10 so I'm supposed to be in the 5th but my parents skipped me ahead to the 6th. I didn't know I was going to the Institute until yesterday. They said I got in at the last minute."

"I didn't know until yesterday either," said Mary. She hopped over a hole in the dock where a plank was missing. "So, you *want* to go to the Institute?"

"Oh yes," answered Elliot, "everyone in my old school —Oceanside Academy Prep—said the Institute was for the smartest kids in each grade. We all wanted to go there. I haven't had a chance to tell my friends yet—they're going to be so jealous. What school did you go to?"

"I've never been to a school," Mary said. "My sister and I always had tutors at my uncle's house. She's 9 and I'm 11, so I guess I'm in 6th grade too. My uncle didn't tell me anything about the Institute." Mary held up her violin case to prove her point. "Do you think *they're* in 6th grade?" She nodded towards Ben and Julee up ahead.

"Probably. Almost all new kids are in 6th grade. I know Henry isn't. He's in 7th." Elliot began to whisper. "My parents told me about him. He's a Kelvin. His family started the Institute, they run the whole thing."

Mary looked down at her feet; they had reached the end of the dock. The sand in front of them shimmered, like millions of tiny stars all piled on top of each other. Ben, Julee, and Henry were ahead, standing in front of a row of bushes that were covered in pink roses. Ben was looking left and right, while Julee was smelling a rose, and Henry was brushing sand off his shoes. The bushes lined the beach as far as Mary could see, like the wall of a fortress.

"I think we'll have to go through 'em," hollered Ben, and he waded into the tangled mesh of waist-high rose bushes. "Watch out for thorns!" A few steps in, he turned around and shrugged. "It's not so bad," he said and then continued on, smiling.

"Not so bad... if you like *thorns* in your pants," muttered Henry.

Julee walked into the bushes behind Ben. "At least it *smells* wonderful," she said.

Henry hesitated, frowning at his shoes and slacks before he too entered the bushes, acting as if they were more like an icky, disgusting swamp.

Elliot and Mary followed. *It did smell wonderful!* Mary thought. The beads jingled on Julee's backpack, and the sound of the surf rolled behind them. All the mist had burned off, and the sun was now shining brightly overhead. Mary's arms didn't feel cold anymore. As she walked through the bushes her summer dress kept getting caught by thorns. She looked up towards the house and pushed her glasses farther up her nose; she could see it more clearly now, now that it wasn't reflecting sunlight straight at her. It was white, and had turrets, and it looked like the houses near her Uncle Edwin's. There was something attached to the top, something like giant plants or antennae, growing out of the roof.

"I wonder what *those* are for," said Julee, noticing the strange objects.

"They look like those things on vines... that wrap around stuff as they grow... what are they called?" asked Ben.

"Tendrils?" Elliot said.

"Yeah, tendrils," said Ben. "They look like giant tendrils."

After passing through the rosebushes, they continued up the trail, over the grassy hillside, and soon, they came to a rock wall, about waist high, that surrounded the house. The space the wall enclosed had row after row of long earthen mounds, like it used to be a garden, but the mounds were overgrown with grasses and wild plants. A gate nearby swung back and forth, its hinges slowly creaking in the breeze. "Looks like the garden needs some help," commented Ben.

They followed the trail alongside the wall and eventually reached the top of the hill, where a stone path led to the front of the house.

The house was two stories high, and square, with a pyramid-shaped roof. The roof, like the whole house, was whitewashed and gleamed in the sunlight, and a metallic spire extended from its top and split into three spiral shaped tendrils. Three turrets, each with a spire and tendrils of its own, were attached to three corners of the square house, and attached to the fourth corner was a large circular-shaped room lined with windows, and topped with a smooth white dome. Vines were growing uncontrolled across the front path, and up the door, and over the windows—some of which were broken.

Ben cupped his hands around his mouth and shouted. "Hellooooo! Anybody home?!" His voice echoed off the stone walls before fading away.

"Hellooooo!" shouted Julee.

"Hellooooo!" shouted Elliot.

They waited… there was no answer.

"Well," Ben said, "I suppose we should knock." He stepped over the vines and approached the door. *Knock… knock…knock.* "Hello!……anybody home?"

They waited… no answer.

"Hellooooo," Julee shouted again.

Ben pounded on the door. *KNOCK KNOCK KNOCK!…*

No answer.

Ben turned and faced the others.   "I don't think anyone's here," he said.

"Ya don't think?" scoffed Henry, who was sitting on the stone wall, still out of breath from walking up the hill.

"I don't think anyone's been here for a long time," said Julee. She kicked one of the vines on the path with her ruby-jeweled boots.

Mary stared up at the house, scanning its white walls and dirty windows. *It's time you learned the truth,* she thought again, and then saw, carved into the stone above the door, and half hidden by leaves, a large spiral letter 'A'— the same design from the forbidden door at her uncle's house!

"Um...GUYS!" shouted Ben, urgently pointing behind them, towards the ocean.

Mary spun around. The boat was speeding away, skipping across the water, its wings outstretched.

"My suitcase!" cried Elliot as the boat rose into the air and climbed higher and higher. They watched, speechless, as the sound of its engine faded away and the boat-plane disappeared from sight.

Mary clutched the violin case and thought of the journal inside. The others were talking rapidly but Mary didn't listen. Whatever was happening was connected to the Forbidden Room, connected to her grandmother. Her mind raced: *it's time I learned the truth—follow the clues—Caroline—Grandma—but Uncle Edwin said she'd died—but she has to be my grandma—why else would the journals be the same—how else would she know who I was—she has to be—she has to be my grandma—she sent me here—*

"Um...Mary?" said Elliot.

Mary was pulled from her thoughts. The others were looking at her, waiting for a response. "Um...what?" she asked, and pushed her glasses farther up her nose.

"What do *you* think we should do Mary?" asked Elliot. She looked afraid, and tears were welling up in her eyes.

Mary knew *exactly* what to do.

She walked straight up to the front door and turned the knob—it was locked. She stepped back and scanned the windows. One of the second story windows on the nearest turret was broken; shards of loose glass still clung to the window frame. She set down her violin case, hopped over the rock wall, squeezed between the house and the overgrown bushes, and shimmied to a large vine of ivy which was growing just below the broken window.

"Mary, what are you doing?" cried Elliot, puzzled.

But Mary didn't answer. She grabbed ahold of the ivy and began to climb. It was just like climbing up to her treehouse. The vines were thick, strong, and untamed, and the leaves shook as she ascended.

"Awesome!" hollered Ben from below.

When Mary reached the window, she wedged her feet into the tangled mesh of ivy and peered into the house. Behind the shattered glass and a crack in the curtain, she saw an open door that led to a bedroom. Piece by piece she pulled the shards of glass away and tossed them into the bushes below.

"Go Mary!" shouted Julee.

When all the glass was gone, Mary wriggled her feet out of the vine, hoisted herself through the window, and tumbled into the room, landing on the floor with a thud.

"Woohoo!" sounded Ben's voice from the path outside.

CHAPTER 6

THE HOUSE OF ANDROMEDA

Mary stood and brushed the leaves off her dress and shook the hair out of her face. The room she had fallen into was small and square and lined with windows. An open door led to the bedroom she had seen from outside, and a stairway descended the turret to the floor below. She poked her head back through the open window and waved at the others. They were all staring at her.

"What's in there?" hollered Ben.

"It's a bedroom, and a stairway," Mary hollered back. "I'll come open the front door, just a minute." She turned towards the stairs—and then something caught her eye—something moving in the bedroom. She froze and listened...

"Hello?" she called, as she crept towards the bedroom and peeked inside. The room was long and narrow, and well-lit from the large windows on the west wall. A royal blue rug ran across the floor to another door at the room's far end. There was a four-poster bed, a dresser, and a large desk, all made of dark, rose-red wood, and carved with detailed patterns of spirals and stars. On the desk was the most beautiful armillary sphere that Mary had ever seen—bigger than the one in her Uncle Edwin's parlor, and more complex than the one in his library.

As she walked towards it, there was a flapping of wings and a loud *squawk*. "Ahhhh," Mary screamed, and shielded her face as a large bird came at her head. It brushed against her hair as it flew to a nest in the eaves of the turret.

"*Squawk...Annie...Squawk...Annie...*," it cried.

Mary uncovered her eyes and looked up—it was a gray parrot. She pushed her glasses farther up her nose. The parrot cocked its head and stared back.

"Did you just say 'Annie'?" asked Mary.

"*Squawk*," said the bird.

"Hey Mary, what was that?" Julee's voice came in through the open window. "Is everything okay?"

Mary hurried back to the turret window and shouted down, "Yeah, it was just a bird. I'll be right there." She headed for the stairs, and half-way down them, she glanced up at the eaves—the parrot was still watching her. At the bottom, Mary slowly pulled open the door which led into the main house and peeked inside. "Hello?" she called. Her voice echoed in the room.

"Annie," squawked the bird from above.

Mary stepped through the doorway. A row of stone pillars stood in front of her, and beyond these, the room opened wide. Light poured in from all sides. A spiral staircase, right in the middle of the room, wound up and up and disappeared into a hole in the ceiling two-stories above. It smelled like… Mary couldn't place it, but it smelled familiar.

To her left stretched a long wooden table, dishes scattered across the top, and chairs tipped-over on the floor. To her right, against the far wall, was a section of bookshelves, sofas, and armchairs. *It's like an entry-hall, dining room, library, and parlor, all combined into one,* Mary thought. It felt comfortable and inviting, despite the great size of the room and the high ceiling.

Two more doors, like the one Mary had just walked through, were at each corner in the back of the room. *Those must go to the other turrets,* she thought. And on the back wall was a pair of swinging doors, like the ones to the kitchen in her Uncle Edwin's house.

Mary stepped forward again and—there it was! The door to the circular room she had seen outside. It was large, with a spiral letter 'A' carved upon it. It looked *exactly* like the door to the Forbidden Room.

Mary was struck with a sudden desire to open it. *It's time you learned the truth,* she thought. She glanced to the front of the house and saw Elliot through a window, sitting on the rock wall, looking down at her feet, looking scared. *Should I tell them—about the journal—about the Forbidden Room—about Caroline's Corner? No. Not yet, not until this makes sense,* Mary decided, and then walked to the front door, undid the latch, and swung it wide.

Ben hopped up instantly. "Nice climbing," he said and glanced around Mary at the room inside. "Wow, look at those stairs!" He skipped through the doorway, and Julee followed behind—she smiled and winked at Mary as she entered the house.

"Uh... where's Henry?" Mary asked.

"Oh," answered Elliot, "he said he wanted to explore around the house. He went off that way." She pointed and then added in a whisper, "he's kinda grumpy." She stepped inside and handed Mary the violin case, and Mary set it by the door. "Mary, what's going on?" Elliot continued nervously. "Henry says it was just a mistake, and they'll send a boat to get us once he can call his father. Do you think there'll be a phone or something here?" She looked into Mary's eyes.

"Um... I don't know," Mary answered awkwardly and looked away.

"Wow, I wonder what's in *here!*" Ben exclaimed. He was standing by the large door. He tried turning the knob—it didn't move—the door was locked. He traced the carved letter 'A' with his finger. "Look at the detail on this A... that's amazing."

Mary tried not to notice.

Ben turned from the door and nodded towards the spiral stairs. "Hey Jewels, wanna go up there?"

"Wild, we don't know whose house this is," she answered, and then added in a whisper, "what if there's something up there?"

"Like what?"

"I dunno, like a dead body or something."

"Scaredy-cat."

"Am not."

"Then let's go. I'll race ya!" He ran towards the stairs, and bolted up them, taking two at a time, his big backpack bouncing loudly.

"Hey wait up!" Julee shouted. Mary watched them wind up and up and disappear through the hole in the ceiling.

"Woohoo!" Ben's voice echoed down. He poked his head out of the hole. "No dead bodies!" he shouted and disappeared again.

Mary smiled. "I wonder how they know each other," she said, and turned towards Elliot who was standing beside the long table, staring at the dishes still scattered across the top.

"This house is so strange," Elliot said. "Why isn't anyone here?" Tears were welling-up in her eyes. "Mary, what's happening? Why did the boat leave us? What is—" she stopped, speechless, with a strange look on her face, and slowly pointed at something on the wall. "Mary, your name is over here. It says *The House of Andromeda.*"

Above the table, hanging between two large windows, was something that looked like a shield. Painted upon it were four squares, like a checkerboard, two yellow and two purple, and across the top was painted a banner with the words: *The House of Andromeda*. In one of the yellow squares was the same spiral letter 'A', and in the other was a drawing of a telescope. The purple squares were dotted with silver stars.

"Why is your name on there?" Elliot asked, puzzled.

Mary didn't know what to say—she needed time to think. "Don't tell anyone," she answered, in a nervous whisper.

"Why not?" Elliot whispered back.

Mary glanced up the spiral staircase. "Just... don't tell anyone yet... I don't want them to know."

"Don't want them to know what?" Elliot asked. She looked both scared and excited at the same time. And just then, the sound of laughing and heavy footsteps came from the staircase as Ben and Julee came bounding down.

"I'll tell you later," Mary whispered quickly, and then walked away from the shield, reaching the stairway just as Ben leapt off the last step.

"I win!" he cheered, throwing his arms up into the air. "Woohoo!"

"Not fair, Wild, you had a head start!" complained Julee. "I want a rematch."

"No way! I won fair and square!" He glanced at Mary and smiled and then sat down next to Julee on the bottom step.

"What's up there?" Mary asked, hoping to sound casual.

"A bedroom," Ben and Julee said in unison and then looked at each other and laughed. Julee elbowed Ben playfully in the side.

"A big bedroom!" added Ben. "It's cool because the roof is a pyramid so the walls come down to the floor at an angle," he built an acute angle with his hands, "and the ceiling goes to a point. It's painted blue, just like the sky, with clouds and everything."

"And there's paper all over the place," added Julee, "and the drawers are all opened up and clothes are scattered everywhere. Why would someone just leave it like that? This place is weird. It kinda gives me the creeps."

Knock! Knock! Knock!

Elliot gasped. The sound had come from the back of the house, from behind the swinging doors that looked like they led to a kitchen.

"Henry?" Ben wondered aloud. He popped up, jogged across the room, and disappeared through the doors. A moment later, his head poked back through them. "Come on! Henry's found something," he hollered and disappeared again.

The girls followed, and as Mary passed through the swinging doors, she remembered sneaking into the kitchen at her Uncle Edwin's, with her sister, searching for food to hide in her bedroom, for when she would be locked inside it for days at a time.

There was Henry and Ben, looking inside the cabinets that lined the walls. The room *was* a kitchen. There was a long countertop and empty shelves and a sink overflowing with dishes. Copper pots and pans hung from hooks on the ceiling, and against the wall was a wood-burning stove, its doors left open, with white ash piled inside. A big knife lay on a wood cutting board on the counter. At the back of the kitchen there was an open door which led outside, the one through which Henry must have entered.

"Henry said there's another house, down the hill out there," said Ben with excitement.

Henry slammed one of the cabinets closed. "No food, of course," he muttered. "What kind of ridiculous house is this anyway?" He leaned back against the counter and crossed his arms and stood, motionless.

"Well… shouldn't we see if anyone's there… at the house?" asked Elliot.

Henry scoffed and rolled his eyes. "Yes, that's the plan, of course."

Elliot looked down at her feet and tucked her hair behind her ears.

"Hey, come on troop," said Ben, who smiled at Elliot and then turned and led the way out the back door.

As Mary stepped outside, the mountain came into full view. It seemed to get bigger every time she saw it, and its green color seemed to get brighter. It was so vibrant; it reminded her of the moss that grew between the rocks under her treehouse, or the slime that grew in the fountain in front her uncle's house. A small set of wind-chimes, attached to the house just beside the door, rang clear, soft tones in the gentle breeze.

From the back door, leading towards the rock wall that surrounded the house, there was a narrow stone path. They walked along it, past the garden rows that were a jungle of shrubs and ivy, until, when they were half-way to the rock wall, the path opened up into a small oval patio. Around the border of the oval, at even intervals, were twenty-four knee-high stones, long and thin and buried so that they were sticking straight up. They were marked with the numerals one through twelve on one half of the oval, and one through twelve on the other half, and right in the middle of the oval were twelve stepping stones—two rows of six squares each—that were marked with the months in a year.

"I wonder what this is for?" asked Elliot, who was bending down, and running her fingers along the number nine carved into one of the stones.

"Looks like a druid monument or something," said Ben, "like Stonehenge."

Mary had seen something like this before, in one of the books in her uncle's library. "I know, it's a sundial!" She stepped towards the row of stones marked with the months of the year and stood on the stone labeled *August*. "You stand on whatever month it is, and your shadow is like the hour-hand of a clock—it points to the time based on the position of the sun." Her shadow landed between the II and III. "It's about 2:30."

Ben nodded admiringly. "That's awesome," he said.

"Yeah," agreed Elliot and Julee in unison.

Henry looked at his watch. "It's 2:43 and 18 seconds, 19, 20, 21, 22." He smirked at Mary and then briskly turned and continued along the path.

They all followed him to the rock wall, where there was an open gate, and the beginning of a dirt trail. From here, Mary could see down the opposite side of the hill they had climbed from the dock. Her eyes followed the trail, down, through a forest of dark green trees and into a valley where there was a long thin lake made by a dam at one end. The trail crossed over the top of the dam and ended at the base of a tremendous cliff, and there, clinging to the cliffside, was a tall stone tower. Beside the tower, built directly into the rock, were a pair of massive doors.

"It looks like a castle," marveled Elliot.

"Yeah, and look at those doors," added Julee.

"Do you think anyone's home?" Elliot wondered.

Ben plucked a stick of grass and put it in his mouth. "I dunno." He shrugged. "Let's go find out."

CHAPTER 7

THE TRAIL TO THE TOWER

Ben marched in front, down the trail, towards the tower on the cliff. Henry, a few paces behind, kept looking at his shoes and frowning. The ground had nearly dried but there were still a few puddles. Mary imagined each drop of water, called forth by the heat of the sun, rising into the air and drifting off with the breeze. She took a deep breath and savored the fresh air. Julee and Elliot walked alongside her.

"He sure is… excited," said Elliot. She gestured to Ben walking up ahead. "He doesn't seem afraid at all."

"Who Ben?" said Julee. "Yeah… he's like that."

"Hey Julee, how do you two know each other?" asked Mary.

"Me and Wild?   Oh, we went to the same school last year.   Well, part of last year, he didn't come until the end. And, we live in the same area, so we got to hang out a lot this summer.   His mom and my foster mom are friends too."

Mary listened to the *crunch crunch* of their feet on the dirt trail.

"If there's no one down there," said Elliot, "do you think they'll come looking for us?   Maybe one of us should go back to the dock, in case a boat comes.   What if a boat comes and we're not there and it leaves without us?"

Mary's heart jumped.   What *if* someone came—and took her away?   Or what if someone was down there, in the tower, and they sent for a boat?   She couldn't leave, she had to go back to the house, back to that door.

"Well," said Julee, "I'm used to goin' along with Ben. We explore old houses a lot, ya know, all the empty ones in Port Oceanside.   I think he has like a map in his head or something.   We never get lost.   He always knows where to find the alleys and the holes in fences and things.   My foster mom says he's *wise beyond his years*.   I'd trust Wild anywhere."

Elliot looked nervously at Mary.

"Hey Julee, we'll catch up with you," Mary said and motioned for Elliot to stop.

"Okay." Julee shrugged and then started jogging ahead, her backpack jingling.   "Hey Wild, wait up!" she shouted.

Mary spoke earnestly. "Elliot, I think my grandma sent me here. It has something to do with that house."

"You mean... you weren't suppose to go to the Institute?" Elliot looked confused.

"I was but... I don't know. Just before I got on the boat that attendant gave me a journal and said it was from Caroline's Corner, and my grandmother's name was Caroline, and inside the journal it said: *it's time you learned the truth, follow the clues.* My uncle said my grandma was dead, but the handwriting in the journal is exactly the same as my grandma's handwriting."

Elliot thought for a moment. "You did look strange when you opened that package," she said, "like you'd seen a ghost." She looked Mary in the eyes. "It's time you learned the truth about what?"

"I'm not sure yet, but I think it has something to do with my mom." Mary looked away.

"Oh," said Elliot, "where's your mom?"

Mary shrugged. "I don't know. She left me and my sister when I was 5. I don't know where she went."

"Oh," said Elliot, "well... follow what clues... like *The House of Andromeda?*"

"Yeah." Mary nodded. "I need to get back there."

"Well, why don't you just tell the others?"

Mary thought. "I need to know more first. I can't tell them. Not yet anyway. But if there's someone in that tower, or a boat comes, I can't go to the Institute, I need to get back to that house."

Elliot nodded slowly and suggested, "well, what if there *is* someone down there, and they have a clue, or know something about your mom?"

Mary considered this for a moment. "Well, if there *is* someone there, and they call, to take us to the Institute, and I run off, you'll know why."

"Okay," Elliot nodded eagerly. "And if someone *is* there, and you disappear, I'll just say you... forgot something and needed to go back."

Mary smiled, and she and Elliot resumed walking. Elliot was so much like her little sister, Mary thought.

Soon, they reached the forest that Mary had seen from the top of the hill. It wasn't like the forest by Uncle Edwin's house, made of trees with big broad leaves that changed color and fell before winter. The floor of that forest was soft and springy, covered in layer upon layer of fallen leaves from seasons before, and in the daylight, it never felt dark underneath the big oaks and elms and maples.

This forest was different. The huge evergreen trees reached high into the sky and blocked out more sunlight; they were spaced closer together, and when Mary looked up through them, it didn't look like stained-glass windows, but like the inside of a tent, with no hint of the blue sky above. The forest floor was covered in fallen pine needles, and moss, and ferns which grew knee high. It felt mysterious and ancient, Mary thought, like she should whisper, or not talk at all. She walked silently, behind Elliot, gazing through the layers of branches, marveling at the the great width of the trunks.   It was much cooler in the forest, and she felt goosebumps on her bare arms.

"Oops," Elliot blurted out as she stumbled forward. "Watch out for this big tree root, it blends right in with the trail, you can hardly see it."

Mary carefully stepped over the root and then looked up and saw daylight, and water, through the trees ahead. The forest ended at the shore of the lake, but the path continued on, along the top of the dam, to the stone tower. Henry was staring up at it, while Ben and Julee were leaning out, over the edge of the dam, looking at the valley below.

"It must be hundreds of feet down," Ben whispered as Elliot and Mary arrived.

The place had an eerie feeling to it, Mary thought. They were dwarfed by the huge cliffs on one side and the forest trees on the other. The roaring river resounded in the valley, far below, and the wind whistled against the barren stone towers that stood before them. Mary was no longer worried about someone being at the house, she knew the tower was empty—she could feel it.

No one shouted.   Unlike the House of Andromeda, overgrown with ivy and weeds, this place was lifeless—barren and empty and lifeless. There were no ferns or grasses or bushes or moss, just stone and dirt, and the remnants of birds' nests in cracks under the eaves and on the metal bars which covered the windows. A solitary magpie hopped from shingle to shingle high up on the roof.

"This place gives me the creeps," whispered Julee.

"Yeah, me too," added Elliot.

"I wonder what's in *there?*" Ben pointed to the massive doors they had seen from on top of the hill, the doors built right into the cliffside. Upon their rusted red surface was imprinted a symbol, two enormous letters, 'K & W', almost as big as the doors themselves. The door imprinted with the letter 'K' was cracked open. Mary could almost feel the cold darkness of the cave within, seeping out of the crack, day and night, into the world.

"Yeah... I don't wanna find out," whispered Julee.

"Me either," added Elliot.

Henry scoffed and rolled his eyes. "What are you afraid of, new kids?" He turned towards the tower and shouted, "Hellooooo!"

hellooooo... hellooooo... hellooooo... his voice echoed around them, again and again off the bare cliff face, before fading away into the valley and the rumble of the river below.

They waited... there was no answer.

Henry walked briskly towards the tower, his hard shoes clicking on the stone and echoing, like the ticking of a clock. He approached the door and twisted the door handle— it was locked. He scoffed and then looked towards the massive doors; and standing proudly, he strode towards them, slipped through the crack, and disappeared into the darkness.

CHAPTER 8

THE FORSAKEN CAVE

Soon after Henry had passed through the doors, a light turned on behind them, and he popped his head out. "See, what are you afraid of?" he gloated and disappeared behind the doors again.

"Cool... go Henry," said Ben. He trotted forwards and slipped through the crack also.

Julee and Elliot looked at each other nervously and then they both looked at Mary, as if they were waiting for her decision.

"Come on," Mary said, "it can't be that bad, it's probably just a cave." And she marched towards the doors confidently, with Julee and Elliot behind.

Upon entering the cavern, the first thing Mary thought of was the mess of books and journals she had seen in the Forbidden Room, except this mess was not one of paper. The disaster before her was one of twisted metal, shattered glass, and splintered wood. Something violent had happened here. There were broken tables and chairs, bookshelves laying face down on the floor, frayed wires dangling from the ceiling, and shards of glass that reflected the artificial lights above. The cavern was huge.

"Computers!" Henry shouted as he jumped over a pile of glass and began lifting one of the collapsed tables which covered a flat black screen and a jumble of wires. "Help me!" he strained under the table's weight. Ben hopped towards him and helped stand the table upright, and as soon as it was steady, Henry crawled underneath and began collecting the computer parts and placing them on the table top. "When I fix these computers," he said excitedly, "we can use them to contact my father, and get to the Institute."

Ben considered the computers and rubbed his chin. "They look pretty old," he said.

"I can make them work," Henry declared, as he dumped a pile of cords on the table.

"Do you want some help?" asked Ben.

Henry glanced up at Ben's vest and cargo pants and hiking boots. "No, I don't need *your* help," he scoffed and returned to work, hurriedly untangling cords.

He's like a young version of Uncle Edwin, thought Mary. She rubbed her arms—it was cold and damp in the cave. She looked up and saw stalactites hanging from the ceiling. The sound of the river outside mixed with a drip-drip-dripping sound echoing from somewhere in the depths.

"I wonder how deep *this* goes," said Ben. He had walked to the back wall of the cave and was standing in front of a door made of thick metal bars. "Helloooo!" he shouted into the darkness. His voice bounced off the walls of the cavern and echoed back, again and again, from deep inside. "Sounds like it goes pretty far."

"It looks like a jail," said Julee warily.

"Yeah," added Ben, "and it's locked too. Look at these strange symbols." He pointed to a large black lock on the door. The lock had a series of 12 unusual symbols instead of numbers. He grabbed onto the thick bars and tried to shake the door—it didn't budge. "There's no way you could break through that," he said, "I've never seen bars so thick."

"I wonder if it was meant to keep something out... or keep something in," said Elliot.

Mary stared through the bars, into the darkness. She imagined large glowing red eyes staring back at her, and a forked tongue flickering, and the thick scales of a massive serpent, heaving up and down slowly, with each silent breath, patiently waiting for its cell to open.

"This place gives me the creeps," Julee said, staring at something on the floor that was metal and had frayed wires sticking out of it. It looked like a severed robot arm.

"What do you think happened *here?*" asked Elliot who was standing next to a twisted pile of broken cages, the kind made for mice or hamsters. "I wish I hadn't worn sandals," she muttered as she tiptoed over a pile of glass.

"Look, someone was sleeping in here," said Ben. "There are cots and blankets and pillows." He picked up a pillow and fluffed it and threw it back on the cot which was pushed up against the cave wall.

"Ahhhhh" Julee screamed and covered her mouth. Something had scurried across the floor. "It went under there." She pointed towards an over-turned bookshelf.

"What was it?" asked Ben.

"It looked like… a green mouse," Julee replied.

Ben stepped over to the bookshelf and kicked it. A mouse ran out from underneath, towards the back wall, and then slipped between the bars of the locked door and disappeared into the dark tunnel. It was giving off a green fluorescent glow. They stared, speechless—except for Henry, who was busy with the computers.

"Uh… did you just see that?" asked Julee.

"Yeah… was that mouse… glowing?" asked Elliot.

"Kinda looked like it," said Ben. He kicked the bookshelf again. Nothing happened.

"Um, guys," said Elliot nervously. She glanced at Mary. "It's getting late, maybe we should go back to that house up on the hill."

"I'm staying," Henry quickly declared. "As soon as I fix these we can get out of here… and get some food."

"Um… I don't think we should split up," said Ben.

There was silence. Elliot looked scared. Mary had to say something. Uncle Edwin was always keeping secrets and Mary hated it. She didn't want to be like *him*. She had to be honest. "I think I know why we're here," she said suddenly.

The others looked at her surprised. Even Henry looked up from the computer.

"Well, I don't know why *you're* here," she continued, "but I think I know why *I'm* here… it has something to do with that house." She pushed her glasses farther up her nose. "My sister and I opened this door at my uncle's, a door he told us never to open, and inside there were all these journals piled everywhere, about *Evergreen Isle*, and we found one with my grandma's name on it, and my uncle caught us, and said he was sending me away to the Institute, and just before the boat left today, the attendant gave me a journal and said it was from Caroline's Corner." Mary took a long breath. "And my grandmother's name is Caroline and written inside it says, *It's time you learned the truth, follow the clues*, and that door up at the house, with the letter A, is exactly like the door we weren't supposed to open at my uncle's, and—" She took another breath.

"And," Elliot added, "there's a shield on the wall that says *The House of Andromeda* and that's Mary's last name." She looked at Mary and winked.

The cave was silent as Ben and Julee stared, wide-eyed at Mary, and then Henry spoke. "So… basically… you don't know why we're here at all, or how we're supposed to get off this island, or find food, or… anything. Right? You don't know anything that can help us?"

Mary pushed her glasses farther up her nose. "Well, I don't know yet, but I'm going to find out, and I'm going back to that house." She felt her temper beginning to rise.

Henry shrugged. "Suit yourself," he said cooly and went back to working on the computer. "Besides, everyone knows Caroline's Corner, that old lady is always giving things to kids going to the Institute. She gave *me* a journal last year, it was probably the same kind."

"But… what about the House of Andromeda, and Evergreen Isle, and the door?" asked Elliot.

"It's probably just a coincidence, and I bet there are lots of Evergreen Isles, it's a totally generic name, and lots of doors with A's on them."

"But… why would the journal say *It's time you learned the truth, follow the clues?*" said Elliot.

Henry scoffed and rolled his eyes. "I don't know, maybe it means the clues of knowledge to learn the truth at the Institute. Don't ask me, that old lady's crazy."

Mary wasn't going to argue. Henry was just like her uncle, he didn't listen, he didn't believe anything, he wouldn't even look up from what he was doing. Her fists clenched. "Come on Elliot," she said, "let's get out of here."

"Good-riddance," said Henry who then glanced over at Ben and Julee. "And what about you two, do you think Mary is *supposed* to be here? Do you think her grandma *sent* her here?"

Ben thought for a moment. "Well, it makes sense to me," he said and smiled at Mary. "I think we should go look for clues at the House of Andromeda." His blue eyes were bright and shining. Julee nodded in agreement.

"Oh please, come on, really?" Henry scoffed. "You *all* think she is supposed to be here? You *all* think it was planned that we were flown to this ridiculous abandoned island and then left here for dead. You're all ridiculous."

Ben shrugged. "Well, *I* don't know why we're here, but this place is awesome. I mean, there are no parents, or teachers, and no one to tell us what to do, and there are these weird houses, and there's like this whole mystery to solve." He glanced at Mary. "What more could you ask for?"

"And no food, and broken computers," yelled Henry. "You all disgust me. Get out of here! Leave me alone!"

Mary didn't need to hear any more. She turned and walked out of the cave and strode down the path to the top of the dam. She looked down at the valley floor, covered in tall green trees far below. The fresh air was a relief from the stale air inside the cave. She could tell from the angle of sunlight that it would be dark in a few hours—*about dinner time*, she thought. Her stomach agreed.

"That dude is hangry," said Julee, as she and Elliot approached and stood beside Mary.

"Hangry?" Mary asked.

"Ya know… hungry and angry… hangry."

"Maybe we should call him Hangry Kelvin?" said Elliot, giggling.

The laugh reminded Mary of her sister. "I'm hungry too," she said. She missed Cassie.

"Yeah, me too!" hollered Ben, jogging up to the girls. "I thought I saw some apple trees up at the House of Andromeda." He winked at Mary and then suddenly looked bashful and glanced away. "I thought I could bring some back for Henry. He could use something to eat."

"Um," said Elliot, "what are we going to do about food? I mean, if Mary's here on purpose, and we shouldn't be expecting anyone, how are we going to survive." She looked at Ben. "Besides apples?"

"A person can live for weeks without food," Ben answered, "it's water you need to worry about, and we have plenty of that." He nodded at the reservoir beside them.

Elliot didn't seem reassured. She looked down at her feet and tucked her hair behind her ears.

"Come on, let's go," Mary said and grabbed Elliot's hand and smiled, and Mary led the way as they climbed the hill, back through the forest, back to the House of Andromeda.

CHAPTER 9

THE THREE TURRETS

Mary, Julee, and Elliot sat under the swaying branches of the apple trees, just beyond the rock wall of the House of Andromeda. Mary's eyes were closed as the sunshine kissed her forehead. She bit into a large red apple and chewed eagerly. "This is the *best* apple I have *ever* had," she said.

"Yeah, I bet even Henry will like these," added Elliot.

"He doesn't deserve them." Mary opened her eyes and looked at Julee. "Is Ben always so nice?"

Crunch. Julee took a big bite. "Uh huh," she mumbled through a full mouth.

"Mary," Elliot began, "how are we going to get in that door, it's locked remember? Ben tried to open it."

"Well, the one at my uncle's had a big metal key. I bet there's a key somewhere in the house." Mary sat up straight. "You two ready to go?"

Julee sighed. "Just one more minute," she said. "It's so nice out, and this apple is *soooo* good. That door'll still be there." She leaned back against her backpack and closed her eyes and took another bite.

Mary smiled. Julee was so calm, like she was never in a hurry, like she never worried about anything.

"What if we can't find a key?" asked Elliot, looking at Mary with eager eyes. "What if we can't open the door, what do we do then?"

Elliot, on the other hand, was always asking questions, like she was trying to figure everything out ahead of time. Mary shrugged and answered, "I don't know, then we'll break a window. Come on."

Julee looked up with one eye open and sighed. "Alright girl, let's go."

The three girls stood, brushed off their clothes, and headed towards the house. "Should we split up or search together?" asked Elliot as they walked through the gate into the overgrown garden.

"Let's stay together," said Mary, "we can start in the bedroom, in the turret I climbed into. There was a big desk in there, maybe the key could be in a drawer... that's where my uncle kept *his* key."

Before they entered the house, Mary stood in the sundial—it was just past seven o'clock. She led the way through the back door, through the kitchen and the great room, and up the turret steps to the bedroom she had discovered earlier.

"*Squawk,*" said the gray parrot, still perched in the turret eaves.

"Hey it's an African Gray," said Elliot. "They're one of the smartest birds alive. My dad told me once—"

"*Annie!*" the parrot squawked.

Elliot froze and her eyes widened. "Did it just say *Annie?*" she asked, puzzled.

"That's what it sounded like," said Julee.

"That's *my* name," Elliot replied. "My first name. My whole name is Annie Elliot Ki, I just go by Elliot because it sounds older. How does that bird know my name? I didn't think they were *that* smart."

"I have a guess," said Mary, "but I'm not sure yet, come on." She hurried into the bedroom and walked straight to the desk. "I have an aunt named Annie, well, *had* an aunt named Annie. She died in an accident when I was three. I think maybe she lived here."

Mary shuffled through the papers and books and journals scattered across the top of the desk and then noticed a plaque on the base of the armillary sphere. "Hey, it *is* my aunts!" she exclaimed. "*To our beloved daughter, Anne Andromeda. With love forever, G.A. and C.A.*—that's my grandma, C.A.,

Caroline Andromeda." Mary quickly began rooting through the desk drawers, one after another, searching for a key.

"This bed is so beautiful," said Elliot. She was running her fingers up one of the carved wooden posts. "Look at all the spirals and stars."

"Oh, look at this!" exclaimed Julee, admiring a large pink gem-stone on the bedside table. The stone's facets gleamed in the late-afternoon sunlight which shone through the large, west-facing windows.

"We have to find that key before it gets dark," Mary said urgently as she closed the last desk drawer, which was only full of paper.

"Wow, look at these dresses!" Elliot exclaimed from beside the large dresser. She turned and held up a long black dress with a big yellow spot on the front. The yellow spot was a star—a photograph printed on the dress—a yellow sphere with dark sunspots and subtle swirling hues of orange and red. A massive flare was erupting on one side, into the black fabric of space.

"Wow!" said Mary and Julee in unison. They walked to the dresser and all three girls began sorting through the clothes, pulling them out of the drawers and holding them up and admiring them. Most of them had a print of something from space—there was a Saturn t-shirt, and a Moon sweatshirt, and pants with galaxies on them.

"I guess we won't have to worry about clothes anymore," said Elliot, "since the boat left with all our stuff." She put a sweatshirt over her head, pulled it down, and looked at the image of an asteroid. The shirt went down to her knees and past her hands. "Most of this stuff is too big for me, but it'll work." She rolled up the sleeves to her elbows and smiled.

"My *mom's* room!" Mary suddenly blurted out. She tossed the shirt she was holding back into the dresser and jogged to the door at the far end of the room. "It has to be here too!" She opened the door—it was a bathroom. She spun around and ran back towards the turret stairs. "Come on!" she shouted and hurried down the steps, taking two at a time. She ran through the great room, past the long table covered in dishes, to another turret door in the corner of the house. She flung it open and bolted up the stairs to the room above.

The room was nearly the same as the first, with an identical four poster bed, desk, and dresser, except the curtains and the rug were rose-red instead of royal-blue. Mary raced to the desk and began searching. Upon it was a metal frame and a box filled with neatly organized glass prisms and lenses. The papers and books were perfectly stacked, not scattered around like on her Aunt Annie's desk. Mary sifted through them and found a journal. She opened it. Stamped on the first page were the words: *From the Library of Cecilia Andromeda.* She flung the journal closed and ran back out the door, nearly crashing into Elliot and Julee as she bounded down the steps.

"It's my Aunt Cecilia's," said Mary, still running. "The last one has to be my mom's!"

She ran past the kitchen doors to the last turret and stopped. *This is it,* she thought. She looked at the door handle. *She used to stand right here… and turn that knob.* She suddenly wished Cassie were there too.

"Aren't you gonna open it?" Elliot asked, panting, as she and Julee ran up from behind.

"Yeah, I just wish my sister were here," Mary said quietly. She glanced at Julee and Elliot and then slowly opened the door—the turret was the same as the others. They walked up the stairs together and entered the room above.

Like the two other rooms, there was a bed, a dresser, and a desk. The curtains and the rug were yellow. On the desk was only a lamp—no books or journals or paper. Mary stepped towards it and opened one drawer, and then another, and another. They were all empty. "There's nothing here," she said, puzzled. She quickly walked to the dresser and opened each drawer… all empty… except for the last one. In the bottom drawer was a purple backpack. Mary picked it up. Attached to one of the zippers was a lanyard strung with little metal spirals and yellow beads. On the beads were painted purple letters which spelled out the name:

V-E-R-A

"Cool backpack," said Julee.

Mary twisted the beads between her fingers. "I wonder how long she lived here." She sat on the bed and began unzipping the pockets.

Elliot sat down beside her. "Mary?" she asked, "how come you never knew about this place? What happened to your mom anyway?"

The backpack was empty, and Mary zipped the pockets closed. "I lived with her until I was five," she answered, "and then one day she dropped me and my sister off at my Uncle Edwin's house, and we never knew why. He never talked about her, no matter how much we begged him, he wouldn't say anything. He would always get so mad. I stopped asking a few years ago. He was married to my Aunt Cecilia, but she died in an accident, along with my Aunt Annie, and my dad, when I was three."

"What kind of accident?" asked Elliot.

"I don't know that either. I don't anything about my dad except that his name was Albert. And I only know that because I overheard my uncle talking about him and my grandma once. That's how I know her name is Caroline. He said that she was dead too, but I don't believe it anymore." She paused. "I don't know what to believe anymore."

"Well, why did your mom never call you or let you know where she was?" asked Elliot.

Mary stared at the purple and yellow beads and shrugged. "I don't know." She looked out the window at the fading light. "Maybe it's too late to find the key tonight."

Julee, who had been sitting at the desk, stood and said, "Ya know what? I'm hungry. Hey Elliot, you wanna go pick some more apples before it gets too dark?"

Elliot shrugged. "Yeah, sure. You wanna come Mary?"

Mary pushed her glasses farther up her nose. "Oh, no thanks, I think I'll just stay here a while."

Julee led the way out of the room, and Elliot followed. As she passed through the door, Elliot turned and asked, "Hey Mary?"

"Yeah?"

"How come your last name isn't the same as your dad's?"

"Oh." Mary smiled. "I asked my uncle that once. He said that in our family, the Andromeda name is passed down through the women. His last name is Edwin Andromeda, and my dad became Albert Andromeda; I don't know what their last names were."

Elliot considered this for a moment and then asked, "Hey Mary... the accident that you said... killed your dad and your aunts... do you think it could have happened on this island? Do you think that's what *It's time you learned the truth* means?"

Mary nodded slowly; the thought had crossed her mind a few hours ago, back at the cave. "Yeah... maybe... I think so."

"Come on Elliot, it's gettin' dark," came Julee's voice from the bottom of the stairs.

Elliot smiled at Mary and then turned and left the room. Mary listened to the footsteps on the stairs and then the sound of the back door opening and closing.

She lay down on the bed, closed her eyes, and listened. The house was still and quiet. She heard the faint sound of the ocean surf, and a gust of wind that swirled around the walls of the house, and then the notes of the wind-chimes ringing outside the kitchen down below.

She imagined her mother as a child, in this room, sitting at the desk, or sifting through clothes in the dresser, or lying on the bed and listening to the ocean. She took a deep breath and sighed. *Where are you, Mom?* she thought.

And then suddenly, Mary remembered! It rushed into her mind—she remembered her mother and she remembered wind chimes—the beautiful sound of wind chimes. She remembered lying in her own bed, at dusk, in the house in the mountains, and listening to her mother play the violin. She remembered how the sound of the violin blended so beautifully with the wind chimes outside, and she remembered how her mother would hide a key to the house on the wind chimes.

Mary scrambled off the bed, and sprinted out of the room—down the stairs, through the great room, through the swinging doors, through the kitchen, and out the back door. There, attached to the wall, hanging just above her head, were the wind chimes, and attached to the wind catcher, swaying back and forth in the breeze, was a large metal key!

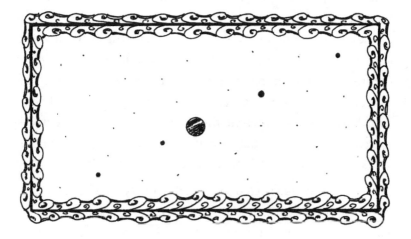

CHAPTER 10

THE OBSERVATORY

A thin metal wire attached the key to the wind-catcher. Mary stretched up, standing on her toes, to reach it. It was coated with rust. *I wonder how long it's been here,* Mary thought. As she untwisted the wire, she imagined the key and the wind chimes flailing and thrashing in hurricane winds. She imagined them hanging perfectly still on hot, summer afternoons. She imagined them coated in ice on winter nights, silenced, and when the sun rose and melted the ice away how the clear notes would ring again.

When she had released the key, Mary hurried back inside. The house was eerie in the dusk—the shadows creeping from the corners, lurking forward against the fading light. She passed through the kitchen, and as she approached the large red door in the corner of the great room, she thought of the forbidden door—how she had opened it nearly a week ago, with her sister by her side. How all this—being sent to the Institute, the journal from her grandmother, Evergreen Isle —it all started after she had opened that door. She knew, somehow, that after opening this door too, the door that stood locked in front of her, that her life would never be the same... and so Mary quickly unlocked it and opened it wide!

She half-expected to smell musty books and see columns of stacked paper on the floor, but there were none. The room didn't smell like paper, it didn't smell like anything. It was empty... completely empty. The bookshelves between the windows were empty, and there was no other furniture— no desks, no chairs, no lamps.

The dim light which came through the windows was a deep red color, and as Mary stepped forward, she noticed the floor was inlaid with beautiful geometric designs—intricate patters of circles and triangles and ovals and rings and spirals. She bent down and ran her fingers across the smooth surface and then—*CLANK!*

She jumped back!

A loud metallic sound had echoed underneath her and above her and there was a loud humming, like the sound of a motor. The floor in front of her was dropping, and the dome ceiling above her was opening from the middle. The thought flashed across her mind that the whole island had been a slumbering giant, and the circular room was the giant's eyeball, and she had awoken it—its eye was open!

Directly in front of her, rising slowly out of the hole in the floor, was a huge telescope. *It's an observatory!* Mary realized. The telescope was supported by a metal frame that was attached to a circular platform, which also held a chair and a small desk. When the dome above had fully opened, and the telescope had ascended, there was a resounding *clunk*... and the room was silent.

Three steps led up the raised platform to the telescope's eyepiece. Mary knew her mother was an astronomer, and her aunts, and her grandma, but she had never looked through a telescope, Uncle Edwin had forbidden it. Everything she knew about space she had only read about in books.

She admired the telescope for a moment—its sleek black surface and great width, as thick as the trees from the ancient forest she had seen earlier that day. She climbed the three steps to the platform. Upon the desk were some papers and a book and a row of buttons and a small screen. Mary squinted in the dim light and could barely make out a series of numbers on the display.

To the right of the buttons was a dial. Mary turned it to the left—there was a loud *clunk* and the whole platform turned, like a carousel, to the left! She turned it back to the right—the platform turned to the right! She felt a sudden thrill of excitement, like she was in control of the island giant —in control of its great eye.

Beside the dial was a small lever. She pushed it up—a motor hummed and the telescope moved up, pointing it higher into the sky. She pushed the lever down, and the telescope moved back down.

Mary grinned and then settled in the chair and stared above her. The half-moon was overhead, and beside it were two bright points of light. She turned the dial a little to the left... a little more... and a little more, and then held the lever until the telescope pointed at the half-moon.

There were two eyepieces on the telescope. Mary looked through the larger one—there was nothing visible but the dark blue sky. She looked through the smaller one and saw a pair of crosshairs and the moon off to the side. *It's a viewfinder,* she thought. Using the controls she carefully maneuvered the telescope until the moon was in the center of the crosshairs. *I wonder if my mom did this?*

She looked into the larger eyepiece—there was the moon! Bigger and more wonderful than she had ever imagined! It was only half lit by the sun, but she could see a faint outline of the dark half. It looked like a perfect ball, just floating above her; like she could just reach out and grab it, and toss it up and down.

On the line between the dark half and the light half, Mary could see, in sharp relief, the features of the lunar landscape: the craters, the mountains, the texture of its surface. If she were standing on the moon, she thought, at that very place, she would be watching the sun set on the lunar horizon, her long shadow cast alongside the shadows of the craters.

For minutes she studied the moon's surface, entranced. *It's another world,* she thought. *A real world.* Mary imagined scooping up a handful of moon dust and letting it sift through her fingers. She imagined jumping high off the surface. She marveled at the tremendous force that kept the moon in orbit around the earth. *Even if the island were a giant, she thought, it would only be a tiny speck compared to the moon.*

She remembered the two points of light shining above, and using the viewfinder and the controls, she maneuvered the telescope towards one of them. When she looked into the eyepiece, she saw a beautiful little ball, wrapped in subtle bands of tan and gray, that she recognized at once. It was Jupiter, with its swirling, striped atmosphere. Four tiny points of light hung next to the planet—Jupiter's four largest moons. They were four perfect, wonderful, little dots, she thought. Mary imagined them in orbit, sped-up, like horses on a carousel, spinning, day after day and year after year, like a clock in space keeping perfect time. She imagined herself standing on the surface of Jupiter, watching all four moons dance around her.

She grinned and then carefully aimed the telescope at the other point of light and looked into the eyepiece. A huge smile grew on her face. It was Saturn. She thought it looked like someone had made a tiny paper cut-out of the planet and taped it inside the telescope. *It's perfect. Its ring is perfect. It's small and plain and colorless and absolutely perfect,* Mary thought. *How far away it must be.* She thought of the sunlight landing on the surface of the moon, and on Jupiter, and shining on her face in the apple orchard just a few hours ago. She wondered how long it took for the sunlight to travel all the way to Saturn, and then back to Earth, to her eyes. Maybe, she thought, the sunlight she was seeing now, reflected off the distant planet of Saturn, left the sun at the same time as the light she enjoyed in the orchard.

Suddenly, Mary felt like Saturn was not so far away at all; she felt connected to it, to Jupiter, to the moon, to all that wandered, together, around the sun. She was a part of it. *Where are Julee and Elliot?* she thought. She had to show them. She turned from the telescope and jumped down all three stairs leading off the platform and ran out of the observatory. "Julee! Elliot!" she shouted. "Where are you?"

The front door opened suddenly. "Mary, what is it?" answered Elliot anxiously.

"I found the key! It's an observatory! You have to see this!" Mary could barely make out the shapes of Elliot and Julee standing in the dark, and then all of a sudden, there was a loud clang and the sound of the motor again.

"What's that?" Elliot asked, surprised.

"Oh no! Why is it closing?" Mary ran back into the observatory and watched, stunned, as the telescope slowly disappeared into the floor and the dome closed overhead.

"Wow... that's cool," said Julee from the doorway. There was a *clunk*, and the observatory was dark and empty again.

"There has to be a switch or something," Mary said. "Help me look." She ran to the wall and began feeling in the dark for anything that might bring the telescope back: a switch, a button, a lever... anything. Julee and Elliot stood in the doorway, motionless. "Come on, we have to bring it back, I have to show you," Mary pleaded again.

"Um...Mary...I can't see *anything* in there," said Elliot, "...show us what?"

Mary continued searching. "Saturn, and Jupiter, and the Moon—they were amazing, I have to show you, you wouldn't believe it."

"Yeah... it's pretty dark," said Julee. "Maybe you can show us tomorrow."

Mary stopped and hung her arms down and sighed. She knew they were right, there wasn't enough light. "Where were you two anyway?" she asked curiously.

"After we picked some more apples," Elliot answered, "we sat on the wall and watched the water as it got dark... and talked. You want one?" She held out an apple. "Where was the key anyway?"

Mary took the apple and spoke rapidly as she left the observatory, walking towards the couches in the great room. "Right after you left, I heard the wind-chimes outside, and I remembered my mom used to hide a key to our house on wind-chimes. So, I went down to look, and there was the key, attached to the wind-catcher, ya know, the thing that swings back and forth and knocks the chimes. After I opened the door, the telescope came out of the floor, and the ceiling opened up, all on its own. I don't know how it happened... or why it closed again." She settled on a couch and looked at the apple and took a bite.

"Weird," said Julee. "I wonder why it just turned on." She glanced nervously around the room. "It's creepy not having any lights," she added.

"The observatory has power," said Mary. "Maybe tomorrow we can figure out how to get the lights to work too." She reclined and put her feet up on the couch and then shivered. The temperature was dropping.

"I wonder if Henry and Ben are alright," said Elliot.

"Hey, at least they have lights down there," said Julee.

"Yeah," added Elliot, "I wonder if they're cold."

"I hope Henry is," said Mary. "Hey, what if we get the blankets off of the beds and sleep out here tonight, on the couches?"

"That sounds good to me," said Julee. "I don't wanna sleep in one of those bedrooms by myself. This place still gives me the creeps, especially in the dark."

Elliot nodded in agreement.

"I'll get the ones off my mom's bed," said Mary excitedly. "There should be enough for all of us." And she swung her legs off the couch, popped up, and skipped to the turret leading upstairs.

It was fully dark now. The only light was the moonlight shining in through the windows. On her way up the stairs, Mary glanced outside. The great mountain seemed bigger than ever, its massive shape silhouetted against the night sky.

In the bedroom, Mary gathered the big quilt, the comforter, and the blankets that were on her mother's bed. *I wonder how long this has just been sitting here, with no one using it?* she thought. With her arms full and the bedding stacked above her eyes, she squeezed through the doorway and floundered down the stairs, bumping into the walls along the way. As she entered the great room, Elliot and Julee laughed.

"You look like... a giant walking mushroom," Elliot giggled.

Mary bumped into the end table and knocked off a stack of books. "Oops," she said, and dropped the bedding in a pile on the floor. "Help yourselves."

The girls sorted through the blankets, and after a few minutes they were lying comfortably on the couches, snuggled under the covers.

"What a crazy day, huh?" said Julee.

"The craziest," replied Mary.

"Just think," Elliot continued, "everyone else who went to the Institute is sleeping on *that* island, in a new place, with new friends, like we were supposed to be."

"I wasn't supposed to go to the Institute," said Mary. "I was meant to come here."

There was silence.

"I hope we don't have to go back into that cave anytime soon," said Julee. "I could never sleep in there, wondering what could be... hiding in that tunnel. I'm scared just thinking about it."

"Yeah, me too," added Elliot. "Let's talk about something else."

Mary yawned. "Let's go to sleep," she said and rolled onto her side and closed her eyes.

"Yeah," said Julee.

As they lay in silence, Mary didn't think about the island, or the house, or her mother, or her grandmother. All she could think about was how big everything was, and how she was small, but she was still a part of it, a part of everything—just like the sun, and the moon, and the rings of Saturn.

"Goodnight," said Elliot.

"Goodnight," said Julee.

"Goodnight," said Mary Andromeda.

Chapter 11

Breakfast

Mary awoke to the sound of knocking. It was morning. Golden sunlight poured into the great room from the large east-facing windows.

"Hellooooo." It was Ben's voice coming from outside. Mary heard the back door open and then, "Hey, wake up! Come here, you have to see this!"

Mary reached for her glasses on the end table, put them on, and saw Elliot rubbing her eyes and Julee yawning and stretching her arms into the air.

"Come on sleepyheads!" Ben shouted from the kitchen.

"Hold on, Wild, we're coming!" Julee shouted back.

Mary cast off her blanket and shook herself awake, and the three girls stumbled into the kitchen, meeting Ben at the back door. He was holding it open and pointing at a box on the ground just outside.

"Looks like we got a delivery last night," he said. "Here, hold the door open, would ya?"

Mary held the door while Ben lifted the box and carried it into the kitchen, setting it down on the counter next to the large cutting board.

"What is that?" asked Julee.

"It was just sitting there, outside the door. It has food in it. Enough for days." Ben started pulling things out of the open box. "Crackers, and cookies, and chips." They all watched, stunned, as he piled the food on the counter.

"Where did it come from?   How did it get here?" asked Elliot. She picked up a jar of peanut butter and began reading the label.

"Is there a note?" asked Mary.

"Not that I can see," said Ben. "Ooh, powdered donuts, I love those!" He swung his backpack off and set it on the floor.

"Did someone just drop that off in the middle of the night," said Julee, "while we were sleeping?"

"I guess so," Ben said, trying to open the bag of donuts. "Maybe it was drone-delivered. That, or there's someone else here, on the island."

"It must have been my grandma," exclaimed Mary. "She's helping us!"

Ben chuckled. "She'd have to be a pretty strong grandma to carry this all the way up from the dock."

"And if it was your grandma," added Elliot, "why wouldn't she come in and see us?"

Mary hopped-up on the counter and took a donut from Ben. "I don't know, but I know it's from her."

"Yeah," said Julee, "this is totally grandma food. When we go to my foster grandma's house on Sunday mornings, we always have donuts, and when we leave, my foster mom always complains that it was unhealthy." She grabbed a donut and popped it into her mouth, whole.

"I got some apples on the way, in case you'd rather have those," said Ben through a mouthful of white powdered sugar.

Julee grabbed another donut and stuffed it into her mouth and smiled.

"Hey," said Ben. He chewed awkwardly for a moment and then swallowed. "So the coolest thing happened last night. I found this big switch in the cave, it was like the size of my arm, and when I flipped it, there were all these sparks—kaboom!—and then this loud banging—bam! bam! bam!—and then this motor sound, like I turned something on, something big." His eyes grew wide with excitement and he tried to imitate the sound, making a sort of grinding, rumbling, squealing noise.

"Wild, that sounds more like a family of giant squirrels," said Julee, laughing.

"...or a train with squeaky brakes," giggled Elliot.

Ben shrugged. "Well, that's exactly what it sounded like, and then Henry started yelling, 'What are you doing!'—or something worse—and he was getting really mad and throwing his arms up in the air, but then all these other lights turned on, around a corner in the cave. That cave is huge! It goes way back, and it was all lit up. There's some crazy stuff in there, like, science fiction crazy: robot parts, and strange symbols, and...," he lowered his voice and leaned in closer, "... weird containers filled with... dead mice." He shuddered.

"Wild, stop it!" said Julee. "I hate it when you do that."

"Well, it's true," Ben continued. "It's like a mad-scientist's cave, like Doctor Frankenstein's. We looked around for awhile, but then Henry got worried about using up all the power or something, so he turned it off, but I think he was just scared."

"Yeah, no kidding," said Julee. "Weren't you? How'd you sleep down there? I wouldn't sleep in there for all the money in the world."

"Eh." Ben shrugged. "It wasn't that scary." He leaned forward again and said in a whisper, "... except for the part with the bats."

"Wild! Stop it!" Julee punched Ben hard in the shoulder. "There are not bats down there. Don't even—" She didn't finish, she just glared at him with a you-better-not-say-it-or-else sort of look.

Ben put his hands up innocently. "What, I'm not kidding, just after dark all these bats flew out of the cave. They came from inside that tunnel, ya know, the one behind the bars."

Julee punched him again.

"Ouch!" He rubbed his shoulder. "Well they gotta eat sometime," he added and backed away from Julee's reach.

"Ben," Mary asked, "what time was that... when you turned on that switch?"

"Just right after dark, how come?"

"Then that's it! That's what opened the observatory! The power comes from down there."

Ben looked puzzled. "Henry said there's a generator in the dam. What observatory?"

"That circular room, it's an observatory. Last night, right after dark, a telescope came out of the floor, and the ceiling opened up, like a big eyelid. It was amazing. But then it just closed again. It has to be that switch. We have to go turn it on again." She slid off the counter excitedly.

"Hold on, sister," said Julee. "We just started eating." She reached for a box of cookies in the pile of food and tore it open. "Girl, you gotta relax, everything's gonna be fine." She handed a cookie to Mary. Mary took it instinctively and sat back on the counter.

"See," Julee said, "you gotta enjoy these moments. It's like my foster mom always says: *enjoy it while it lasts because it never does.*" She glared at Ben. "And don't you start talking in that voice again."

Ben grinned and stuck his tongue out at Julee. "I can go turn on that switch. I'll bring some food to Henry. If breakfast doesn't cheer him up, I don't know what will." He stuffed a cookie in his mouth, swung his backpack over his shoulders, took an unopened bag of donuts in his hands, and said cheerfully, "I'll be back soon." He winked at Julee and turned and left the house.

"Oh, that Wild," said Julee. "Sometimes I just wanna smack him." She slapped the back of one hand against the other.

"I think he's funny," said Elliot.

Mary didn't say anything—she liked Ben—and for a few more minutes they ate in silence.

"What should we do while we wait for him to turn on the power," asked Elliot, "explore the house some more?"

"Let's go up the spiral stairs," said Mary. "I bet it's my grandma's bedroom. It'd be a good place to start."

"Yeah," said Julee, "and there was stuff everywhere. It's a mess."

"There were also some things in the observatory, papers and a book, on a desk by the telescope," said Mary. "With all day to search, we *have* to find something."

"Mary," said Elliot, "if your grandma sent you here, and she's leaving us food, why doesn't she just show up? Why doesn't she just come and talk to us?"

Mary shrugged. "I dunno, but I feel like the sooner we figure out what's going on, the better."

"Well, what kind of clues should we be looking *for?*" asked Elliot.

"I'm not sure," said Mary, "but I think we'll know it when we see it. Anything that mentions my mom."

Julee leaned back against the counter and rubbed her stomach. "Uh, I'm stuffed," she said.

"What should we do about all this food?" asked Elliot. "Should we put it in the cabinets or something?"

"Nah, just leave it there," said Julee, "no one's gonna make us clean up."

"Yeah, we can be as messy as we want," said Mary mischievously, as she hopped off the counter. "Come on, girls." And she headed towards the bedroom at the top of the spiral staircase.

CHAPTER 12

THE LETTERS

When she reached the top of the staircase, and poked her head into the room above, Mary imagined that she was at the top of a beanstalk, about to enter a mysterious castle in the sky. The pyramid-shaped ceiling reminded her at once of the Forbidden Room—painted blue with clouds that looked almost real. It would be easy to forget there was a ceiling at all, Mary thought, if it weren't for the stale warm air and musty smell. It smelled like the attic in her Uncle Edwin's mansion, where she and Cassie would build forts out of old blankets and boxes.

It was messy. The dresser drawers were open and clothes were strewn about. The mattress had been pulled off the frame and lay half on the floor. A desk had been tipped over, its contents scattered in piles nearby. The curtain rods above the triangle-shaped windows were bent or broken, and the purple and white curtains had fallen to the ground. Morning sunlight poured in.

"And my mom says *my* room is messy," said Elliot, gazing about as she stepped off the staircase onto a large purple rug.

"I told you," said Julee from behind, "it's a big messy bedroom."

"Yeah, but look at the ceiling," said Elliot, "how did they do that?" She walked towards the edge of the room and brushed the painted ceiling with her fingers. "I've never been in a pyramid-shaped room before. It feels kinda weird."

"I think I'd hit my head a lot," said Mary. The desk chair lay on its side in front of her. She picked it up and set it aright. "It looks like someone was searching for something, the way the drawers are all emptied."

"Like they were in a hurry," said Elliot.

"Or just didn't care about making a mess," added Julee.

Elliot sat down on the rug next to a pile of books and picked one up. "I wonder if they found what they were looking for."

Mary sat beside her. "I guess we should just look for anything that seems suspicious, or that mentions my mom." She reached for a book that lay upside down on the floor, its pages bent. It was about Neptune.

Julee joined them and they all began searching. There was a journal filled with charts that had something to do with Mercury, there was another that recorded weather conditions, and others about gardening, and planting times, and harvest times, and the phases of the moon.

"Hey, here's a letter to your grandma," said Julee, and handed the paper to Mary. It was addressed *Dear Caroline*. Mary read it. It was about the discovery of a new type of comet and the unusual color of its tail.

"This one is for Galileo Andromeda," said Elliot. "Is that your grandpa?

"Yeah, it must be," exclaimed Mary. Elliot gave the letter to Mary, and Mary read it. "It's something about ordering new lenses for a telescope," Mary said, disappointed.

She glanced around the room and imagined how it must have looked when her grandma and grandpa lived there. She imagined her grandma sitting at the desk, responding to a letter about comets, while her grandpa stared out the window, at the island and the sea, and thought about new telescope lenses. She imagined her mother as a little girl, racing up the spiral staircase with her sisters, shouting and laughing and bursting into the room during a game of chase, or jumping on the big bed. She wondered what her grandpa was like... if he would have scolded them and sent them away or joined in the laughter.

"Hey, look at this," said Elliot, curiously. She was unfolding what looked like a large black map on the floor. "It's a picture of stars and a woman chained to a rock." Mary and Julee moved closer while Elliot read. "It says, *The*

Constellation of Andromeda: The Chained Princess. Named after the beautiful princess Andromeda, who was chained to a rock by her parents, king Cepheus and queen Cassiopeia, and offered as a sacrifice to be devoured by a terrible sea-monster. She was eventually rescued by the great hero, Perseus."

"Whoa," said Julee, "that's messed up."

"Yeah, I know that story," Mary said. "My sister and I used to pretend we were the characters. Which was easy, ya know, since we're named after them." She cracked a smile and then stared back at the drawing of the princess chained to a rock. "That's how I felt at my uncle's, like I was just chained up, waiting to be devoured... or rescued... or either way, it wasn't up to me."

"Well," said Julee encouragingly, "now you're Mary Andromeda, The *Un*-Chained Princess." And she gave Mary a gentle punch on the shoulder and smiled.

Mary smiled back. "We still don't have any answers though. I wish we knew what to look for." She stood and walked to the window and looked down at the green rolling hills, at the path that led to the dock and the shimmering blue sea. "Why did they leave?" she wondered aloud. "It's so beautiful here." She thought she saw a dolphin jumping far out on the water.

"Hey, listen to this," said Elliot. "It's about something called the Royal Fellowship Society."

Mary spun around. "That's what my grandma's journal was about, the one at my uncle's."

"It looks like it's been ripped out of something," Elliot said. She gave Mary the ragged page.

Mary read it aloud:

"We, the founding members of the Royal Fellowship Society, for the betterment of all humankind, hereby dedicate our lives to the pursuit of Science. We promise to freely share, among all members, our wealth and our knowledge. We shall protect this knowledge and prevent any use of it which could lead to the destruction or suffering of people or nature. We agree to fund the development of research estates on Evergreen Isle, which must be kept secret and always remain self-sufficient. In matters of disagreement, we vow to abide by a majority ruling among members of the Society. Signed,

Caroline Andromeda, Galileo Cassini Andromeda,

Democritus Dalton, Marie L. Dalton, Emmy Euler,

Archim—

—and the rest has been ripped off," Mary finished.

"So," began Julee, "your grandparents built this house, on this island, to do science, in secret?"

"Yeah, I guess so," said Mary.

"It said, *research estates,*" began Elliot. "Do you think there could be other houses here, besides this one, and the one by the cave?"

"Yeah, maybe," answered Mary. "The rest of the signatures are missing. Who knows how many there could have been."

"Oh, this island gives me the creeps," said Julee. "Why isn't anyone here anymore? Why did they just leave it all? Something bad happened here, that's for sure."

Mary looked at the page again. "It says they were doing research *for the betterment of humankind,* and not for *destruction or suffering.*" She shrugged.

"Maybe whatever happened was an accident," said Elliot. "Maybe something went wrong."

"The accident that killed my dad?" wondered Mary. She pushed her glasses farther up her nose. "Come on, let's keep looking."

They continued searching near the desk and found more notes about the estate garden and letters about astronomy, but nothing more about the Royal Fellowship Society. They searched the rest of the room—under the clothes and sheets and in the dresser. They set the desk upright—there was nothing underneath, no hidden compartments or secret drawers. They lifted the bed back onto the frame and made it. They folded the clothes and put them back in the dresser, and put all the papers back in the desk drawers. They found nothing that seemed like a clue.

"I'm hungry," Mary sighed after a time and flopped on the bed. "We've looked everywhere."

Elliot sat beside her. "We haven't looked under the rug," she offered. "I always hide stuff under the rug in my room." She leaned down, grabbed the corner of the purple rug and flung it up.

There, laying on the bare floor, was an envelope!

"Go Elliot," cheered Julee.

Elliot smiled, and Mary quickly scooped the envelope up and tore it open. "They're letters!" She unfolded them carefully and scanned the pages. "From my mom... to my grandpa! They were written when I was five, look." She pointed at the date in the corner before reading:

Dad,

Please leave the island. Mom and I need your help. It's getting worse. He's spreading lies about us and threatening us. We don't know what to do, Dad. Frances and Neil have joined him. Their calling themselves 'The Union of Power'. He won't listen to Ada, he won't listen to me, he won't listen to Mom. You might be able to reach him. He respected you more than anyone. Please, come to us. If we can't stop him soon, we may never stop him. Please, Dad.

Love, Vera

"Stop who?" wondered Elliot.

Mary shrugged. "I don't know." She shifted the pages and read the next letter:

Dad,

Please help us! Please come. Please leave the island. Michael has joined them. Michael! It would have broken Albert's heart. We have to stop him, but we don't know how. He's so convincing. He lies and makes promises and — he convinced Michael, Dad. He's recruiting everyone. We have to expose him. Time is running out. Come! Please!

Love, Vera

"Who's Michael?" asked Elliot.

"I dunno," Mary replied, "but he must have been someone close to my dad." Mary shifted the pages and read the last letter:

Dad,

Hide everything, like we planned, and leave the island. I beg you. Mom is begging you. He will come for you Dad, and take you, and find out what you know. You wouldn't recognize him anymore. He won't listen to reason. Don't try to talk to him. Don't underestimate him. Please, Dad. There is nothing he won't do to keep it a secret. Nothing. The girls are not safe with me anymore. You're not safe on the island. For my sake, for Mom's sake, for your granddaughters' sake, leave as soon as you can. Don't come to us. Go where no one can find you. Hide everything and leave! Please, Dad.

Love, Vera

Mary slowly set the letters on her lap.

"Keep *what* a secret?" asked Elliot.

"I don't like this place," said Julee nervously. "Something really, *really* bad happened here."

"Whatever it was," said Mary, "my mom knew about it, and so did my grandpa—something they weren't supposed to know—or something this person didn't *want* them to know."

"Maybe it was about the accident," said Elliot. "Maybe it was this person's fault, and your mom and your grandpa knew the truth..."

"She was in danger," said Mary. "That's why she left me... to protect me... to protect me and Cassie. That's why my uncle would never tell us."

"Do you think she's still in danger? Do you think she's hiding somewhere?" asked Elliot. "Maybe she was captured, or maybe she was kill—" Elliot gasped and covered her mouth with both hands.

"I know she's alive," said Mary. "I know it. She may be in hiding, or she may be captured, but I know she's alive."

"I wonder if your grandpa left, or if he got caught," said Julee. "She said this guy would do anything to keep it a secret. Hey, maybe that's why this house is all messed up, because someone was looking for... whatever your grandpa was supposed to hide."

"My mom said she needed to *expose him*," added Mary. "Maybe that's why I'm here. My mom and grandpa knew the truth about the accident, and it's hidden somewhere on this island. My grandma sent me here to find it, and expose whoever caused it."

"Then your mom... won't be in danger anymore," added Elliot, "and she can come out of hiding... if that's where she is."

"But why you?" asked Julee. "Why would your grandma send you, and not someone else?"

Mary's mind raced. "My mom said to *hide everything, like we planned.* Maybe it's hidden where I would find it, but no one else would, like the key on the wind-chimes. And maybe this was my grandma's only chance to send me, before I was stuck at the Institute."

CLANG!

A loud metallic sound echoed from down in the house —the same sound that Mary had heard last night. The observatory was opening again.

CHAPTER 13

THE RIDDLE

Mary ran down the spiral stairs, carrying the letters from her mother to her grandfather, the page about the Royal Fellowship Society, and the star chart that Elliot had found with the constellation of Andromeda. At the bottom, she could see the clear blue sky through the door to the observatory. "Hey, I'm gonna go get my mom's backpack so I can put all this stuff in it, I'll meet you there." She ran to the turret and up the stairs to her mother's bedroom.

Laying on the floor by the dresser was the purple backpack. She kneeled down, unzipped the large pocket, and placed the papers inside. "I'm gonna learn the truth, Mom," she said out loud. "I promise." She stood up tall, swung the backpack over her shoulders, and ran out of the room towards the observatory.

Julee and Elliot were already there, staring up at the great telescope that had risen from the floor. Through the open ceiling came the sounds of the surf and of gulls squawking in the distance. The warm fresh air smelled like the sea.

Now, in the daylight, Mary saw that the windows were stained-glass—purple and yellow and green and blue and red —beautiful patterns of triangles and circles within circles. She wondered what the room would look like, with the dome closed, and light coming in through the colored glass alone.

"There has to be some way to open and close this without flipping a switch in that cave," Mary said, her eyes scanning the walls. "There has to be a switch in here."

"I wonder where all the books went," said Elliot.

"Yeah," said Julee, "every other room has been so messy, except for this one."

"… and my mom's room," added Mary.

"Hey, what's that?" said Elliot curiously as she walked towards a bookshelf. "There *is* something here… it's a book… but it's not." She moved something on the shelf, and a motor hummed, and the dome ceiling began to close, and the telescope began to descend into the floor. "Oh no!" she squeaked and jumped back. "What did I do?"

Mary ran towards her. On the bookshelf, standing upright, was a book, but it was only a book from the front. From the side, it was a long piece of metal that disappeared into a hole in the shelf. "Hey, it's a hidden switch," said Mary. "Well, it's not hidden now, but if this shelf were full of books, it would blend in perfectly." She ran her fingers along the fake book that made up the front of the switch. It was dark leather with gold-colored printing that said *The Starry Messenger*.

"Cool," said Julee.

"I'm so sorry," said Elliot nervously, "I didn't mean to." There was a clunk as the dome closed and the telescope settled into the floor.

"That's okay," Mary said, "I bet it'll—" she stopped, speechless, as she turned and faced the open room. The light, filtered through the stained-glass, was landing on the floor and the walls in an explosion of colors and patterns. The dome ceiling above, painted like a sunset, seemed to glow with a light of its own; the yellows and oranges and reds and golds of the clouds swirled and blended together, like they were moving.

"I feel like... I'm inside a rainbow," whispered Julee.

"... or a kaleidoscope," whispered Elliot.

"... or fireworks," said Julee.

"... or a cathedral," added Mary. She slowly stepped forward into the center of the room. Colors from all sides enveloped her. She held her arms up in the air and closed her eyes and spun around. The changing colors flashed and danced over her eyelids as an enormous smile grew on her face.

"I wanna try," whispered Elliot. She stepped forward and began spinning alongside Mary. Julee followed, and all three girls spun, in silence, amidst the ever-changing colors in the Andromeda Observatory.

And then laughter and a voice came from the doorway. "Hee hee... what are you girls doing?" It was Ben.

Mary stopped spinning and smoothed her dress over her legs and pushed her glasses farther up her nose. She felt like her face was turning red.

"Wild, don't sneak up like that!" scolded Julee.

Ben smiled. "Sorry," he said, trying not to laugh. He gazed up at the ceiling. "Wow... how did they do that?"

Mary skipped to the bookshelf. "We found a switch. Look at this." She showed Ben the fake book and the hidden lever.

"Open it, Mary," said Elliot.

Mary pushed against the fake book—the motor started, the ceiling opened, the floor dropped away, and the telescope grew in its place.

Ben watched with wide eyes. There was a *clunk* and the room was silent. He nodded approvingly and whispered, "Awesome."

"Hey, where's Henry?" Elliot asked. "Did he like breakfast?"

Ben swung his backpack off and set it on the floor. "Yeah, that helped a little, he's pretty frustrated about those computers though. He's still down there, trying to fix 'em. He keeps sayin' he can use 'em to contact his father so he can get to the Institute. I don't know, they seem pretty old to me." Ben shrugged and then reached down to get something from his backpack. "He did get *this* to work though." He pulled out a camera and held it up to his eye and pointed it at the ceiling, pretending to take a picture. "I found it in the cave... it's pretty cool." He turned the camera over in his hands and then returned it to his backpack.

"We found out why these houses are here," Elliot said eagerly. "Mary's grandparents were in this thing called the Royal Fellowship Society, and they built these houses, to do science, in secret. And we think Mary was sent here by her grandma to find out about the accident that killed her dad. Show him the letters, Mary."

Mary opened her mother's backpack, took out the letters and the page about the Royal Fellowship Society, and handed them to Ben. As he read, she climbed up the steps to the telescope platform, scooped the papers off the desk, and returned to the observatory floor. "Let's see what's in here," she said and sat down crosslegged. Julee and Elliot sat beside her.

There was a book titled *A Catalogue of Nebulae*. Mary paged through it. It was written in a different language and was filled with dates and numbers.

"That's French," said Elliot. "We were learning it at my old school."

Mary closed the book and set it aside. There were a few loose papers, also filled with numbers, and a journal that looked old, like the one from Caroline Andromeda. Mary fanned the pages... it was blank, completely blank.

"Is that it?" asked Elliot.

"Yeah, looks like it," said Mary.

"Where are the clues?"

"I dunno." Mary shrugged.

"Hey, let me see those papers," said Julee. She took one of the papers from Mary and held it up to the light and examined it closely.

"What are you doing?" asked Elliot.

"Looking for secret messages... I saw it in a movie once." Julee looked at each page carefully against the light. "No... no secret messages." She shrugged and set them down again.

"Whoa," said Ben who had just finished reading the letters, "whoever this bad-guy is sounds like a... bad guy. I wonder who he is, and if your grandpa ever got off the island, and... hey, maybe there's a bunch of other houses here." He had a glimmer in his eyes. "I wanna go exploring," he said, with such a sense of excitement, Mary thought, that he could convince anyone to go with him.

"You know how it says *hide everything, like we planned,*" said Elliot, "we think Mary's grandpa hid something, that's what *it's time you learned the truth means,* and left clues so that only Mary would find them, that's what *follow the clues* means."

Ben nodded. "Makes sense."

Mary looked down at the empty journal and the book in French. "Why aren't there any clues here?" she said, frustrated.

"Can I see?" asked Ben. Mary handed him the book and the empty journal. He flipped through them. "Yeah, looks like an empty journal... and a book in French... and some writing in the margin." He shrugged.

"What writing in the margin? Where?" said Mary, surprised.

"Right here." Ben held open the *Catalogue of Nebulae* book and showed it to Mary. Written sideways, in scribbled cursive, was what looked like a poem. Mary read it aloud:

> *When the next Andromeda,*
> *upon her throne does stare,*
> *at her reflection she will see*
> *the answer will be there.*

> *Hiding up among the stars,*
> *among the black of night,*
> *wait patiently for what may come*
> *of faint and distant light.*

"That's mysterious," said Elliot, when Mary had finished.

"Yeah, what's that supposed to mean?" asked Julee.

"It sounds like a riddle," said Ben.

Mary thought. She read and re-read the riddle in her mind.

"Mary?" Elliot asked.

"*The next Andromeda,*" Mary answered, "that's me, or it could be my sister... and *her throne*... I bet that's the chair by the telescope... and *her reflection*... that's the constellation of Andromeda.   It means... the answer is hiding in the constellation of Andromeda, *among the stars*... and I can find it, with the telescope."

Elliot looked puzzled. "What can you find by staring at a constellation?" she asked.

"I dunno." Mary shrugged. "Maybe I'll remember something, like when I heard the wind-chimes."

"Ya know what this means?" said Ben, standing up excitedly. "It means we have all afternoon to explore, ya know, while we wait for dark."

"After we eat something," added Julee.

"And use the bathroom," said Elliot.

Mary thought for a moment. She felt like she was missing something, like she needed to search the house again. "I don't think I'll go... I wanna stay here and make sure we've found everything."

"Well," said Ben, "do you want me to stay? I will if you want."

Mary smiled and shook her head. She felt like her face was turning red again. "No, that's okay, just let me know what you find."

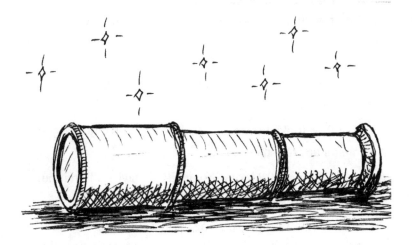

CHAPTER 14

THE CHAINED PRINCESS

While the others were gone, Mary, alone, searched the rest of the house.

She carefully searched each bedroom—her Aunt Annie's, and Aunt Cecilia's, and her mother's—looking under the beds and behind the dressers and underneath each long, colored rug. She searched the kitchen cabinets and under the couches and the couch cushions. She flipped through all the books on the bookshelves in the great room. She dragged a chair from the long dining table and, standing upon it, she peered on top of the high bookshelves in the great room and in the observatory. She even walked around the house, twice, searching the walls and under the shrubs. She found nothing that seemed like a clue or that mentioned her mother or the accident.

In her Aunt Cecilia's desk she found a spyglass—a small telescope that could extend and then close up again. Mary imagined a pirate captain, standing tall at the wheel of his ship, the wind whipping his hair, using the spyglass to scan the horizon; and she imagined Cassie, held prisoner, tied to the mast with thick rope and a gag in her mouth. She imagined swinging down from the rigging—with a cutlass in hand—hacking through the rope, disarming the pirate captain, reclaiming the stollen spyglass, and commandeering the ship —with its ruthless pirate crew—to tropical islands and buried chests filled with treasure.

She smiled and put the spyglass in her backpack.

Under her Aunt Annie's bed she found a thick book of star-charts—maps of the entire sky. Each page had descriptions and drawings of constellations and notes on important stars or unusual objects. The page that Elliot had found, of the Andromeda constellation, had been taken from this book.

In the kitchen, Mary discovered that some of the cabinets had been a home for mice—their little black droppings mixed with bits of gnawed wood and fluffy dead grass. She found a drawer of old spices and bins for sugar, salt, and flour. The sugar was gone, the salt was fused together, like someone had mixed it with glue, and the flour had bugs in it. Mary gagged at the sight of them and quickly covered the bin again.

Hours went by. She picked up the dining table, tucking in the chairs and bussing the dirty and dusty dishes to the kitchen sink. Water came out of the kitchen faucet, but it was brown, and only came in a trickle.

By late-afternoon, Mary was standing in the kitchen, wondering if she should walk down to the lake to get some water, when she saw Henry out the window. He was walking towards the house, slowly, and he was glancing all around at the garden rows, as if he were interested in what was growing there. He was smiling. He didn't look at all like the irritable, arrogant boy that scoffed and said *ridiculous*.

When he reached the back door and entered the kitchen, Mary stood at the counter with her arms crossed. Henry noticed her and straightened up, and his smile disappeared. For a moment he furrowed his eyebrows and scowled, but then he looked away, out the window, and spoke in a matter-of-fact voice. "I fixed the computers, but there is no way to communicate off the island. I came for more food." He glanced at the counter, where the food was piled, and his eyes opened wide. "So… you think your grandmother left this?" he asked.

"I *know* she did," answered Mary.

Henry's eyes squinted through his glasses and he stared at Mary, as if he were trying to decide whether or not she was lying. Mary stared back.

"Can I have some?" he finally asked.

Mary pushed her glasses farther up her nose. She squinted back. "Fine," she answered.

Henry began digging hungrily through the pile of food. His face brightened as he pulled out a bag of chips, opened it, and leaned back against the counter. "Where are the others?" he asked smugly and crunched down on the chip in his mouth.

"Exploring the island," Mary replied. "I was just going to the lake to get some fresh water." She walked to the faucet and turned the handle.

Henry watched the brown water trickle out. "If you let that run, it will come out clear... eventually." He crunched another chip. "It's brown from sitting in the pipes for years. It's just rust."

Mary frowned. "How long will it take?" she asked calmly.

Henry shrugged and grinned in a know-it-all sort of way. "Let it run and we'll see... won't we?"

The water trickled down the sink and Mary remembered the sword-fight she had imagined with the pirate captain. She imagined sword-fighting with Henry, disarming him, and making him plead for mercy with the point of her rapier at his throat. She heard voices outside and saw Ben, Julee, and Elliot walking towards the house, laughing, their long shadows bouncing along behind them.

crunch... Henry ate another chip.

Elliot spotted Mary through the window and ran ahead. She burst into the kitchen. "Mary, look at these shells I found." On her hand were four small shells—oval and iridescent colored. "They reminded me of the observatory."

Her eyes beamed and she glanced over at the sink. "Hey, why is the water running... and why is it brown?"

"Henry thinks it'll turn clear if we let it run awhile," Mary answered, and then asked, excitedly, "what'd you find, any other houses?"

"No." Elliot shook her head as she put the shells in her pocket.

"But we found some more cliffs," said Ben from the doorway. "We went back to the shore, by the dock, and walked north along the beach until we came to these huge cliffs that went right into the water. These giant waves were crashing against them. Bam!" He smacked his hands together like waves hitting rocks. "I don't think it'd be safe to swim around 'em, the waves are too strong, you'd be tossed against the rocks and probably split open like a melon." He grinned and made an exploding motion with his hands, and Julee punched him in the shoulder.

"Ouch!" He stuck his tongue out at Julee. "Anyway, if we're gonna find out what's on the other side of those cliffs, we can't go around 'em, we'll have to go over 'em, through the forests. Man am I hungry." He licked his lips and walked to the pile of food like he was hypnotized.

"Mary, did you find anything here?" asked Elliot.

"No, just some more star charts, and one of those folding telescopes, and some... well... let's just say... don't look in the flour bin." Mary shuddered.

"Bugs?" asked Elliot.

Mary nodded and grimaced.

"I don't mind bugs." Elliot shrugged.

"Ick," said Julee, and she shivered her hands, like she was shaking off imaginary insects.

"Hey Henry," said Ben happily, "did you fix the computers yet?"

Henry squinted his eyes. "Yes, but they can't communicate off the island. They're too old."

"Well... at least they work with the camera." Ben bobbed his head up and down. "I took some pretty sweet pictures of the beach today."

Henry rolled his eyes and looked away.

"Hey Mary," Ben continued, "did you tell him about the RFS—that's what we're calling it now, the Royal Fellowship Society—and the Andromeda constellation?"

Mary shook her head no.

"Can I?" Ben asked.

Mary nodded half-heartedly.

"Well..." Ben began to tell Henry everything—about Andromeda, and the island, and the letters, and the riddle. Mary walked back to the sink and watched the water flowing down the drain. It was clear. She put her hands under the faucet and let the thin stream of water run through her fingers. It was cold. She cupped her hands and let them fill up with water and she drank. It was wonderful. She drank more and more, handful after handful, until her stomach started to hurt.

When she had finished drinking, and Ben was done talking, she stood up tall and looked at Henry. "You were right," she said calmly and wiped her chin dry.

Henry squinted at her. "So what do you think you'll find by looking at a constellation?" He spoke like he still didn't believe any of it.

"I don't have to explain it to you," Mary replied.

"Suit yourself." Henry grinned and took an unopened box of crackers from the stack of food on the counter and walked to the door. On his way out he turned and chuckled. "Don't stay up too late… *princess,*" he said and left the door open behind him. Mary scowled as he walked away.

"I know he wasn't just hangry that time," said Julee. "That boy is *mean.*" She turned to Ben. "You don't have to be nice to him ya know."

Ben shrugged and put his hands in his pockets.

"Why doesn't he believe you, Mary?" asked Elliot, puzzled.

"He's just like my uncle," Mary muttered. "He doesn't believe anything."

"Well," said Julee, "we'll just have to show him then, won't we?"

Mary smiled. She imagined Henry, cold and wet and starving, standing in a downpour, banging on the kitchen door, begging to be let in, begging for forgiveness.

"Can we go sit down," asked Elliot wearily, "we've been walking all afternoon."

They moved into the great room and settled on the couches as Elliot relayed more details of their hike, with frequent smiling and nodding by Julee, and additional mumblings of "it was awesome," by Ben, along with some sound-effects and bird noises. At one point, Julee left for the kitchen and returned with a jar of peanut-butter and a box of crackers and she made a large pile of peanut-butter cracker sandwiches, which they ate eagerly.

As the daylight faded, Ben returned to the cave—against Julee's wishes. He said he didn't think anyone should be alone at night, and that he'd be back in the morning. When the girls moved into the observatory, Mary opened the dome ceiling and raised the telescope. Two points of sunlight, the light reflecting off Jupiter and Saturn, pierced the fading blue sky. The moon was no longer beside them—it had moved slightly to the east, and its surface was just over half-lit now. Mary took out the star-chart of the Andromeda constellation from her backpack and unfolded it on the floor.

"So... how will we know where to point the telescope?" asked Elliot. "It's not like there are really pictures up there."

"We can find it," Mary pointed at the chart. "See, it's in the northern sky. There's the north star, and there's Andromeda, it looks like a long skinny V; and right next to it is Cassiopeia, Andromeda's mother, which looks like a W; and there's Perseus, the hero, which kinda looks like a Y. Once we find Andromeda, we can aim the telescope, like I did last night. Let me show you."

Mary climbed up to the platform and settled in the chair. "Stand back," she announced before turning the dial on the control panel. The motor hummed and the platform turned.

"Wow!" exclaimed Elliot.

"Yeah... wow is right," added Julee.

"And this lever moves it up and down, see?" Mary moved the lever up, and the telescope moved up. "I can point it at anything I want. And this little eyepiece is the viewfinder, so I can aim it perfectly before looking through the main eyepiece. Wanna see? I think there's room for both of you up here."

Elliot and Julee climbed up onto the platform. It was crowded.

"How about... Saturn first?" Mary said. Looking at the sky, she maneuvered the telescope until it was pointing towards Saturn and used the viewfinder to position it exactly. "Go ahead and look." She stood up and let Julee sit in the chair.

Julee peered into the eyepiece and then jumped back. "No way!" she exclaimed, her eyes wide open. "Is that for real?"

Mary smiled and nodded.

"Let me see, let me see," said Elliot, bouncing up and down and side to side.

Julee stood and Elliot sat down and peered into the eyepiece...

"Uh...I don't see anything," she said, puzzled.

"Here, let me look," said Mary.

Elliot stood and Mary sat down and peered into the eyepiece...

"Oh, it's moved out of view... or rather... we've turned away." Mary positioned the telescope and stood up and Elliot sat down and peered into the eyepiece...

"Uh... I still don't see anything."

Elliot stood and Mary sat down.

"Okay, here you go." Mary stood up and Elliot sat down and peered into the eyepiece....

"Uh... still nothing," said Elliot.

"It keeps moving out of view. Here, try and use the controls to "

Elliot spun the dial and the platform spun to the left like a carnival ride. "Oops." She spun it back to the right and they spun to the right. "Oops again." She chuckled nervously, and after a long time of jolting left and then jerking right and then left and then right, the telescope was pointed in a completely different direction than where it had started. "I'm not very good at this," Elliot said bashfully. "You better do it." She stood up, and Mary sat down, and in a few moments the telescope was pointed at Saturn again.

"There *has* to be a way to track something," said Mary, "so we don't have to keep moving the telescope, so that it follows the sky automatically."

"Well," said Julee, "what about this big button that says TRACK?" Her finger was hovering directly above a large button on the control panel labeled TRACK.

Mary and Elliot looked at it... and then at each other... and then at the button... and then laughed. When Mary had positioned the telescope, yet again, she pushed the TRACK button, and watched for a moment. Saturn stayed fixed, right in the center of view. The telescope was moving—slowly, precisely—fixed to the sky above as the Earth turned below.

Elliot finally saw the beautiful ring of Saturn, and Mary showed them both the surface of the Moon and the moons of Jupiter. The sky darkened, and the light from more and more stars shone down upon them. The girls gazed upwards in silence.

"Just look at the Milky Way," marveled Julee after a time. "You don't see *that* in Port Oceanside."

"Hey Mary," said Elliot, "I don't see anything that looks like a chained princess. What should we be looking for again?"

"It kinda looks like... two lines... like a long skinny letter V... or two legs," Mary said.

"Hey Mary, before we look at Andromeda, can we look at the Milky Way in the telescope?" asked Julee.

"Sure." Mary shrugged and pointed the telescope to a bright patch of the Milky Way and looked—

It was stars! The Milky Way was stars! The wispy, cloudy light that arched across the sky was made of stars—packed so tightly, so close together—thousands and thousands of them. "There are *so* many," Mary whispered. She beamed at Julee. "Look."

Mary suddenly imagined her little sister, spinning on a merry-go-round, but the spinning disc was made of stars—tiny stars, with black space in between—going around and around. She imagined running along side it, laughing, and then reaching out and grabbing 'hold and hopping on. Around and around. She imagined the spinning disc growing bigger and bigger until she and Cassie were just tiny specks, with a vastness of stars and space between them.

"That makes me feel small," said Julee as she pulled away from the eyepiece.

Mary smiled, and Elliot started bouncing again and pointing excitedly. "Oh, oh, oh... I think I found it. Right there, below those other stars that look like a W."

Mary followed Elliot's outstretched finger. "You're right! And that's Cassiopeia, and there's Perseus."

"It doesn't look like a woman to me," said Elliot. "Once I stopped looking for pictures, and started looking for dots connected by invisible lines, I could totally see it."

"Way to go Elliot," commended Julee.

Over the stick-figure constellation of Andromeda, Mary imagined a terrified princess, shaking with fear, trembling in the shackles that pinned her forever to the black sky.

"So... what are you going to look for?" Elliot asked.

"I don't know," said Mary, "I guess I'll just look over the whole thing in the telescope, and see what happens." Mary turned the controls and aimed the telescope towards Andromeda and peered in the eyepiece...

Julee and Elliot silently waited.

Mary moved the telescope again.

Julee yawned. "I'm tired, I'm gonna go sit on the floor," she said and yawned again.

"Yeah, me too," said Elliot, and she and Julee descended the stairs and settled against the wall while Mary continued her search.

She directed the telescope, bit by bit, scanning the constellation, searching the stars. *There are so many of them,* she thought, countless tiny specks of light, so many more than she could see with her naked eye. She searched... and searched... and searched, waiting for a clue, or a sign, or a memory.

The stars reminded her of nothing.

Henry is right, what could I possibly find by looking at a constellation? she thought after what seemed like an hour of staring. Her head was starting to hurt. She sighed and took-off her glasses and rubbed her eyes.

"Mary, what is it, what did you see?" asked Elliot tiredly from the floor below. Julee was sleeping, curled up beside her.

"Nothing... I don't see anything... just stars... and some blurry spots." She rubbed her eyes again. "My eyes are tired."

Elliot stood slowly. "But... where's the clue?"

"I don't know... maybe there isn't a clue... maybe we were wrong."

Elliot yawned. "Well... what do we do now?"

Mary stared blankly at the observatory wall. "I don't know... let's just go to bed... maybe we'll think of something tomorrow." She came down the steps, walked to the switch, and pushed it—the motor hummed... the observatory closed... *clunk.*

The noise woke Julee, who mumbled something about the Milky Way galaxy, and the three girls sleepily stumbled to the couches in the great room and crawled under the blankets.

As Mary drifted off to sleep, she imagined the mythical princess Andromeda, fighting at the chains that bound her wrists, struggling, frantically, as a grotesque sea-serpent slowly emerged from the dark water, its mouth open, its fangs gleaming, its black eyes fixed upon her. She imagined the princess, cowering, huddled close to the bare rock, her face turned away as the monster slithered ever closer. She imagined the king and queen, Andromeda's parents, watching in silence from the cliffs above as the waves crashed, and the terrible serpent slowly devoured their daughter, limb by limb.

Over and over the scene played in Mary's mind until, at last, she fell asleep.

CHAPTER 15

SAND AND GRASS

Mary awoke.

knock—knock—knock

"Helloooo," Ben was shouting from the back door.

The three girls were sprawled out on the couches. Julee was snoring softly, and Elliot was face-down in a pillow.

Mary put on her glasses and slowly shuffled to the kitchen. Ben, in his green pocket-covered vest, with his big backpack strapped to his shoulders and the camera slung around his neck, smiled and waved at her through the window.

"Did you find anything?" he asked eagerly as Mary opened the door. He walked straight to the pile of food and began digging through it.

"No... nothing," said Mary, and she grasped the curls that were dangling on her cheeks and tucked them behind her ears. "There was nothing there."

Ben looked into her eyes. "Well...," he said, trying to sound encouraging, "do you wanna explore the island today?" He looked back at the food. "Maybe we'll find something. I was thinking we could go back to the beach and head south this time—since north was an impasse. Oh yummy, want some muffins?" He opened a box and took out a muffin wrapped in plastic.

"Yeah," Mary answered, "that sounds good."

Ben paused. "Er... about the muffin or heading south?" He smiled.

Mary smiled back. "Both," she laughed.

The swinging doors flung open. "Wild, you wake up too early," said Julee, yawning. She noticed the muffins, and Ben tossed her one over the counter. He tossed one to Mary also.

"You better eat fast," he winked, "we're gonna go *south* today."

Julee pretended to glare at him while she very slowly unwrapped the plastic and very slowly brought the muffin to her mouth and very slowly took a bite and chewed... very slowly.

The swinging doors opened again, and Elliot stumbled in, rubbing her eyes. Her black hair was sticking straight out on one side. "What's going on?" She yawned and hoisted herself onto the counter.

"We're gonna explore again," said Ben, "south along the beach."

"Oh, I like the beach," said Elliot happily. "Mary, are you coming?" Mary nodded and Elliot's eyes brightened. "We can look for shells!"

Mary smiled. She turned to Ben. "Is Henry still in the cave?"

"Yeah, he's trying to fix something else now. I think he really likes it in there, with all those broken parts and gadgets. I doubt he'd want to explore the island with us."

"Well that's good," said Mary, "I wouldn't want him to come anyway."

After their fill of breakfast, the three girls went to Annie Andromeda's dresser to look for clean clothes. Most were too big for Elliot, but nearly everything fit Julee, and only the floor-length dresses were too long for Mary. Elliot kept her jeans but traded her floral-print t-shirt for a big white shirt that had blue stripes; she tied a knot in the shirt so it wouldn't hang down past her knees. Julee traded her colorful summer-dress for khaki shorts and a red t-shirt with yellow and orange spots that looked like splattered paint, and Mary changed into a knee-length summer dress that was light-purple covered in little yellow stars. There was even a drawer of clean socks.

Julee gathered all their dirty clothes and took them to the kitchen sink and washed them lightly with dish soap and then draped them over the shrubs outside to dry. She offered to wash Ben's clothes too, but he said he could wait another day, he was ready to explore.

Ben and Julee both had water bottles, which they filled and put in their backpacks, along with the jar of peanut butter, two boxes of crackers, the rest of the powdered donuts, and four apples that Ben had brought from the orchard. The food went into Julee's and Mary's packs because Ben's was already full.

"What do you keep in there anyway?" Elliot asked.

"Oh, ya know, survival stuff—a big knife, and a pocket knife, and a fire-starting kit, a compass, a poncho, a hammer with an axe on one end, a medium-sized knife, scissors, and pliers, a first-aid kit, a water-purifier, fishing hooks, some empty bags, a little shovel, rope, toilet paper, a flashlight with some extra batteries, a tarp... and... that's it, I think." He nodded happily.

"Yeah," said Julee, "I used to think he was a little crazy for carrying all that stuff around, but now we might really need some of it."

Ben's eyes sparkled.

As they left the house, Mary closed the door behind them. She looked up at the mountain—its snow-capped summit glistened in the morning sunlight. She followed the others around the house, beside the rock wall, and down the grassy hillside, on the path towards the dock.

Mary watched the rolling ocean waves on the horizon and listened to Elliot talk about home and her parents and her old school and her friends and movies she'd seen and books she'd read and places she'd been and animals she liked. Mary was glad that Elliot did all the talking.

After they had passed through the dense wall of wild roses and had reached the beach, they walked south. The sand high on the beach was loose and formed dunes that were a struggle to walk through, but the sand close to the water was wet and packed firm. They all walked there, just above the white foam of the surf, except Elliot, in her sandals and rolled-up jeans; she scanned the beach for shells and other curious sea-things as the waves lapped against her feet.

After a time, the beach-line turned and the dock was gone from view, behind the grassy hills. Julee was quiet, but she looked happy, and Ben constantly scanned the hills and the horizon, like he was trying to remember everything. Every so often he would stop briefly, aim his camera at something, and take a picture. Mary could never tell exactly what he was taking pictures of.

When the sun was getting high in the sky, they stopped and ate all the donuts and drank a whole bottle of water. Ben stared south along the beach line, shielding his eyes. "Looks like more cliffs," he said. "If we can't get around 'em, we could cut across the hills, and make our way back to the house in a big loop. Some of those hills are pretty high, I bet we could look out and see more of the island."

They continued along the beach, and soon, Ben was proven right. The flat beach ended abruptly at the base of high cliffs, where powerful waves crashed against boulders that had fallen from above. Huge masses of rock, covered in cracks and still clinging to the cliff face, looked poised to fall at any moment. A constant squawking and babbling from the sea-birds, which sat in countless dirty nests built on the cliff, mixed with the sound of the waves. Mary could feel a light spray of water, carried by the wind, from where the ocean, wave after wave, relentlessly battered the rocks.

"Yeah, there's no way we're going around that," said Julee, decidedly.

They sat close to the cliff, in the cool spray, and ate peanut-butter crackers and nearly finished the water. Elliot kept looking up nervously at the rocks dangling above. When they had finished, they climbed up a steep, sandy ravine onto the grassy hillside above the beach. From here they could see the border of an evergreen forest. The trees stretched from the top of the ocean cliffs, along the hilltops to the east, and disappeared behind the taller, grass-covered hills to the north.

"I bet that connects to the forest by the cave," said Ben. "Looks like we'd have to go through it to see what's on the other side of these cliffs." He scanned the surrounding hills and pointed to the tallest grassy hill in the distance. "I bet that's the tall one you can see from the House of Andromeda... shouldn't be that hard to reach it." Mary surveyed the terrain... gentle, grassy, rolling hills.

They walked up a hill... and then down the other side... and up another... and then down the other side... and another, and another, and another. It was hot. The grass was itching Mary's legs. The curls that hung on her cheeks and shoulders were damp with sweat.

As she took off her glasses and wiped them dry, she thought that Ben alone still looked happy to be exploring.

Elliot hadn't said anything since the third hill, and Julee's smile was gone. Mary wanted to whine, *are we there yet?* but she didn't. As she walked, she recited the riddle in her mind, in rhythm with her footsteps:

When the next Andromeda,

upon her throne does stare,

at her reflection she will see

the answer will be there.

Hiding up among the stars,

among the black of night,

wait patiently for what may come

of faint and distant light.

When the next Andromeda...

She said the words over and over again, and soon, as if little time had passed at all, they were standing on the top of the tallest hill, the one they had been walking towards.

The white roof of the House of Andromeda was visible in the distance, not far to the north. The great mountain loomed behind it. To the east, the forest blanketed the hills and disappeared into the valley below; and beyond the forest rose the massive cliffs Mary had seen two days ago. The very top of the Stone Tower was visible, behind one of the green hills in the foreground. The cliffs looked like an impenetrable barrier. To the west and south, the grassy hills rolled down to the ocean, which shimmered in the afternoon light. Mary surveyed the route they had taken, up and down, over the hills. It was a long way, she thought.

Ben figured it would take a few hours to get back to the house, and since the clouds that had been building overhead didn't look like storm-clouds, they might as well rest for a while. While they rested, they drank the last of the water, and ate the apples, and the last of the peanut-butter crackers. Julee licked the jar of peanut-butter clean.

Mary slung her backpack onto the ground and lay down on the soft grass and gazed up at the sky. It was a beautiful clear blue spotted with bright, white, fluffy clouds. She saw faces in them: a silly face with puffed out cheeks and a big bulbous nose, an angry face with furrowed eyes and a sharp chin, a laughing face with an open smile. As she stared at the laughing face its smile grew bigger and then stretched apart and it looked like a face with two mouths, and then the two mouths were the eyes of a different face that was upside down and looked like an old women with a crooked nose, and then the nose got smaller and the old women's mouth grew longer and it looked like the face of a bird with its beak turned to the side.

click

Mary glanced over at Ben. He was sitting in the grass holding his camera. Julee was lying on her back, a few feet away, her eyes closed, and Elliot was bent over, on her hands and knees, staring wide-eyed at something in the grass.

click

Mary closed her eyes—patterns of circles and lines and a faint purple glow quivered on the back of her eyelids. She listened to the gently blowing breeze and the click of the camera...

click

"Whoa... that's cool," said Ben.

"What?" asked Elliot.

"This dial here... I can change the shutter speed."

"Shutter speed?... like when you shake back and forth if you're scared?" asked Elliot.

Ben chuckled. "No, the shutter, the thing in the camera that opens and closes to let light in. Ya know, that clicking sound that it makes, ka-chik, that's the shutter, opening and closing, really fast. If it's open too long, then too much light is let in, and the picture is all white, or blurry. My mom taught me about it."

"Oh... well... why would you want to change it?"

"I dunno, the camera usually does it automatically, depending on how much light there is. But it's cool that I can change it if I want. If I turn it all the way over here and hold down this button—click—the shutter just stays open until I let it go—click."

"Oh... but wouldn't that make the picture all white and blurry?"

"Well, yeah... unless it was really dark and the camera was really still. I bet you could take some neat pictures of fire... or stars."

Mary's eyes popped open. "Wait, what did you just say?"

"Uh... that you could take pictures of fire or stars?" answered Ben, confused.

Mary sat up straight. Her mind raced: *upon her throne does stare—wait patiently—hiding—faint and distant light—stare—stare.*

"Mary, what is it?" asked Elliot.

"Ben, could we attach the camera to the telescope... in the observatory?"

Ben's eyes widened. "Maybe... what are you thinking?"

"If we could attach the camera to the telescope, and do what you just said, hold the shutter open, then we could take a picture of Andromeda. The riddle says I have to *stare* and that the answer is *hiding in faint and distant light*. If we use the camera, it will be like staring at Andromeda, and we can see the light that is too faint to see with our eyes—all the light will be collected in the camera. Maybe *that's* what I have to do."

"Yeah!" Ben nodded excitedly... and then looked away and frowned.

"What... what is it?"

"Um... well..."

"What?"

"Well... we'd need Henry's help."

"Why? What would we need *him* for?"

"To see the picture on the computer. I don't know how to do it... and the computer is kinda *his*... or... he fixed it."

"Okay. So what? We have all the food. He'll have to help us or he can't have any."

Ben paused and thought. "Yeah... okay... you want me to ask him?"

Mary stood up decisively and slung her backpack over her shoulders. "No. I'll do it," she said. "Come on."

Julee opened one eye and sighed.

They walked quickly, with Mary leading the way over the grassy rolling hills, back to the House of Andromeda. At one point, Elliot spotted what looked like a cluster of white bushes on a distant hillside, but when the bushes started to move, everyone agreed they were sheep. Mary counted exactly twenty-eight by using Cecilia Andromeda's spyglass, which she still had in her backpack.

In a small pond, which was nestled between two of the hills, Ben thought he saw fish that no one else saw. He vowed to come back later and catch one and prove himself right.

When they finally reached the house, the sun was low in the sky. Mary stood in the sundial—her shadow pointed to 6. She followed the others, wearily, into the kitchen.

"Welcome back," came Henry's voice from the corner. He was sitting on a chair, one he had brought from the dining room table, and he was eating. "Did you find any clues... princess?"

CHAPTER 16

THE AMAZING EYE

Mary didn't waste any time. She stood tall, with her arms crossed, and stared straight into Henry's eyes. "I need your help," she said proudly.

A grin slowly grew across Henry's face. He squinted. "You need *my* help, do you?"

Mary stared back. "Yes."

Henry took another bite of whatever he was eating, chewed, and swallowed. "Well, what is it?" he said casually.

"Will you help me?"

"Now, that depends on what you need, doesn't it?"

"I'll tell you what I need when you agree to help me."

Henry squinted even further, until his eyelids were open no more than a sliver. "Okay... *princess*... what do you want?"

"I need your help with the camera. I need to attach it to the telescope, and take a picture of the Andromeda constellation, and then see it on the computer. *That's* what I want."

Henry chuckled. "And... you think this is part of the quest from your long-lost grandmother, do you?"

"Yes," Mary declared.

Henry laughed again and then stood and glanced at his watch, as if Mary had been keeping him waiting, as if he had much better things to be doing. "Well, let's go then, shall we?

Ben took the camera from around his neck and handed it to Mary. She took it and walked, determined, to the observatory. When the telescope was lifted, and the dome ceiling was opened, she turned to Henry. "Ben said that we could keep the shutter of the camera open, for as long we wanted, and take pictures of stars."

Henry reached for the case. He removed the camera and quickly started pushing buttons, and switching switches, and turning the camera over in his hands, and opening and closing little flaps on the sides, and dismantling pieces of it. "It's just like any camera, clearly," he said. He carried it up the stairs to the telescope, sat down, and began twisting on the telescope eyepiece.

In less than a minute, he relaxed back in the chair, with his hands folded behind his head. "Would you like to see, princess?"

Mary climbed the stairs and stood behind him. The camera was attached to the telescope eyepiece; flashing numbers appeared on the camera's display.

"This is a timer," he said, pointing to the numbers. "You use these arrows to set the time that the shutter will be open, and then you push enter." He looked at Mary. "Think you can handle that?"

Mary glared back.

Henry chuckled and then spoke slowly, like he was explaining something to a baby. "Tomorrow... you will unscrew the camera... and then bring the camera to me. Can you handle that too?"

Mary continued to glare.

"Aren't you going to say thank you?" Henry smirked.

"Henry," Julee said sharply from the floor below, "get outta here."

Mary felt a rush of pride. She smiled at Henry, and pushed her glasses farther up her nose, and stood poised. "Thank you Henry, that will be all," she said politely, and graciously motioned for him to leave. "I shall bring the camera to your gloomy cave in the morning. Thank you ever so much."

Henry scoffed, rolled his eyes, stood, and stepped down off the platform.

"Please help yourself to as much food as you'd like," Mary called as he passed through the observatory door and walked out of sight. Elliot started giggling, and then Julee joined in, and Ben, and soon they were all laughing out loud.

"I could have done that," Mary said. "All he did was screw the camera onto the telescope."

"Yeah," said Ben, "and I knew about the timer."

Mary glanced at the camera and the flashing numbers on the display. "How long should we set the timer for, do you think?"

"I dunno," Ben thought for a moment, "an hour?"

Mary nodded. "Yeah… okay… an hour, if the picture comes out too light or dark we can always try again tomorrow night."

Mary stepped off the platform, and they all moved to the kitchen. They hadn't eaten since the tallest hill, hours ago, and for the rest of the evening, they ate and talked and ate more. Elliot talked about her parents, Julee talked about the four different foster families she had lived with, and Ben talked about how he and his mom had moved every year since he was born. He could remember seven different houses in different parts of the world: three in cities, two in the country, one in the desert, and one in the mountains. Mary told them all about her Uncle Edwin's mansion, and her treehouse, and her sister.

The more they talked, the more Mary realized how her life had been so different than theirs—she had almost never been allowed to leave her uncle's house, and the only other person she really knew was her sister. Julee had lived with one family that had nine children and another with six, Ben had made friends all over the world, and Elliot had friends from school and a mother and a father that loved her. The only person that loved Mary was her sister... and maybe her mother, wherever she was.

She imagined Henry, saying she was ridiculous for thinking her mother loved her. She remembered her Uncle Edwin saying *she left you, little girl.* She remembered her mother, driving away, and her sister, standing there watching, only three years old, crying "Mommy! Mommy! Don't go!"

"Mary, are you okay?" asked Elliot.

Mary sat up straight. "Yeah... I just hope this works, using the camera with the telescope... that's all."

Julee put her arm around Mary's shoulder. "Well if it doesn't, then we'll just keep trying, won't we."

As night approached, like the night before, Ben left for the cave and Mary, Julee, and Elliot went into the observatory. Mary wanted to sleep there, so that if it rained while the telescope was out, she could wake up and close the dome ceiling. They moved couch cushions and pillows and blankets onto the observatory floor and watched the sky darken, and when there was no hint of light but from the shining stars above, Mary tracked the telescope to the center of the Andromeda constellation and entered one-hour on the camera timer.

click

Mary took a deep breath. "Well... I guess that's it." She shrugged and rejoined Julee and Elliot on the observatory floor.

"Hey Mary," said Elliot, "ya know how you call your eyes your naked-eyes, when you're not using a telescope or anything?"

"Yeah."

"Well, you have glasses, *and* a camera, *and* a telescope. Your eyes are like... super-eyes."

"Yeah," added Julee, "you're like a super-hero. Introducing... the Incredible Mary Andromeda and her Super-Spectacular-Amazing-Eyes."

Mary smiled. She imagined the island-giant, like a great big lovable cyclops, lying on its back and staring into space beside them. *Mary Andromeda and the Amazing Eye*, she thought to herself. She liked it.

As she fell asleep, The Amazing Eye continued to stare. Faint and distant specks of light entered it, one by one, and were caught in the camera, captured forever on a photograph.

Mary blinked... and her eyelids slowly closed... and soon she had fallen asleep and into a dream...

✧ ✧ ✧

She was in a desert; her sister was beside her. The sky was red. They trudged, hand in hand, towards a horizon of dark clouds that flashed with lightning. Wind picked up the sand and pelted it, like needles, onto her bare legs. Her dress flapped violently, and her hair whipped her face, and she struggled to breathe.

"Mary, where are we going?" Cassie shouted over the howl of the wind. Mary turned to answer but Cassie was gone. She looked down at her dress and it was still. The wind had stopped and Mary was standing before a massive steel door, with a rusted spiral letter 'A' pressed upon it.

She touched the door softly with her finger and it swung open with a creak. Inside was blackness. Infinite, unending, blackness. She stepped through the doorway and squinted her eyes and peered into the dark. She felt like the darkness was expanding, and like she was expanding with it. Gradually, points of light began to shine, one by one, like stars, lighting up, one after another after another, filling in the blackness faster and faster until all the lights together had turned the space completely white.

Then, in just the same way, points of darkness began to appear, like black stars in a white sky, one after another, faster and faster until the space was again completely black.

This same thing happened, again and again, black points in white space and then white points in black space, and faster each time, until there was no change at all between blackness and whiteness, there was only a still and solid gray.

Mary heard a seagull, and the sound of the surf, and smelled the ocean, and the grayness disappeared, like a fog lifting, and Mary was on a beach, sitting on a tree-swing. The sun was shining and a gentle wind blew against her face as she swung back and forth, and back and forth. She turned her head and beside her, chained to a rock at the base of a huge cliff, sleeping peacefully on the ground, was the princess

Andromeda. Beside the princess, also sleeping, coiled up, was a sea-serpent, no bigger than a snake.

Mary felt something around her neck and saw that she was wearing a chain necklace with a large key dangling upon it, but the key wasn't there, it was an empty hole of blackness shaped like a key. She stared at it, puzzled, wondering how she could use the key-shaped hole to unlock the chains of the princess when she heard her mother's voice, gently calling, "Mary... Mary," from the sea in front of her.

Her mother, with her straight blond hair and blue eyes, was standing, a few steps away, knee deep in the water, smiling and reaching out. Mary jumped off the swing and ran towards her with outstretched arms, splashing through the water, laughing, but with every step that Mary took, her mother moved farther and farther away, into the ocean. "Mom!" Mary shouted, "come back!"

Mary ran quickly back to the shore, hoping to reverse what she had done, hoping that when she turned around, her mother would be only a few steps away again, but when Mary looked, her mother was still out in the water, swimming and smiling.

Mary ran towards her again. But again her mother moved farther out to sea and began thrashing her arms like she was struggling to swim. Mary ran frantically back to shore and turned and ran towards her mother a third time. Her mother, far out in the water now, struggled and screamed, and soon she was gone, drowned, behind the rising and falling of the waves.

"Mom!" Mary cried, and the ground started shaking violently and the cliff rocks began to fall from above, crashing and crumbling on the beach. Then, there was Cassie again, standing a few steps away, smiling and waving in the shallow water, oblivious to the enormous boulder falling through the air directly above her head. "Cassie!—" Mary shouted out, as the boulder fell and hit with a sickening crunch.

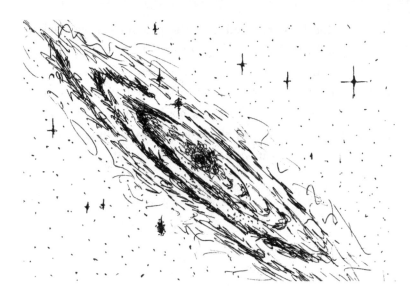

CHAPTER 17

THE HIDDEN IMAGE

Mary awoke, sweat-covered and trembling. She looked around her. She was lying on the observatory floor; the light of dawn was overhead; Julee and Elliot were asleep beside her; the picture was finished. "Wake up," she shouted, and hurriedly slipped on her shoes, rushed up to the telescope, and unscrewed the camera.

"What's wrong?" Elliot said, blearily rubbing her eyes.

"Come on, wake up, let's go!" Mary set the camera into its case, zipped it closed, slung it around her neck, and ran towards the door, grabbing her backpack on the way out.

"Mary, wait up." Elliot hollered from behind.

Mary ran through the house and out the back door—past the sundial, past the garden rows, past the rock wall. She ran down the dirt path, holding the camera tightly. The vision of her sister, crushed under a boulder, and her mother, drowning in the ocean, replayed in her mind. She ran faster and faster.

She looked down and watched her legs flashing below her as she entered the dark evergreen forest. She scanned the trail for rocks and holes and roots. The great trunks of the towering trees rushed by her.

She ran—her sister crushed under a boulder, her mother drowning in the ocean. She looked up—there was the lake, just ahead, and the dam, and the cliffs—

She looked back down—her foot caught a root—she tripped—she flung forward—she flew through the air—hands outstretched.

She hit the ground and rolled—once, twice. Her arms and knees and shoulders and face plowed through the dirt.

There was a crunch and the sound of breaking glass and she slid to a stop. The camera was crushed, pinned underneath her.

"No, no, no!" Mary cried and frantically untangled the twisted strap around her neck. She unzipped the case—tiny bits of glass, like diamonds, lined the black fabric inside.

"No," she gasped. She looked at her hands, they were covered in dirt and blood. She remembered falling from the tree swing, her mother washing her hair, washing the blood out, her mother's beautiful naked eyes, smiling, the water running through Mary's hair, washing the blood away. She imagined her sister, crushed on the beach, and her mother, gasping for air, arms flailing, drowning in the ocean.

"Mom," she cried and began to shake. She dropped the case and hugged her legs and trembled. Twigs and pine-needles clung to her clothes and blood ran down her shin. She heard footsteps.

"Mary, are you okay?" shouted Elliot. "Mary, what's wrong? Mary? Oh no—" Elliot ran up and knelt down beside her. "Mary, what happened?"

"It's broken... the camera is broken," Mary shivered.

"Oh Mary, your leg," Elliot gasped, "and your shoulder."

Mary's right knee and shoulder were deeply scraped, covered in blood and dirt and pebbles that had buried into her skin.

"Oh Mary." Elliot picked out a twig that was dangling in Mary's hair.

"It's broken, Cassie. The camera is broken. We'll never find her. Never."

Elliot looked puzzled and then reached her arms around Mary and hugged her. "It'll be okay Mary. It'll be okay."

"Hey, what's wrong?" Julee shouted from up the trail.

"Mary fell... she's hurt..." Elliot shouted back.

Julee ran up to them and glanced over Mary's wounds. "Let's get her to the cave. Ben has a first-aid kit. He'll know what to do. Mary, can you stand up?"

Mary nodded, and with Julee's help, she stood slowly. Her left ankle throbbed and the skin on her right leg, shoulder, and face burned with pain.

"Can you walk?"

Mary put her weight on each leg. "Yeah," she said, "but my ankle hurts."

"Hold on to me," said Julee.

Mary nodded. She limped slowly, leaning on Julee's shoulder, while Elliot carried the broken camera. Ahead was the stone tower, vacant and lifeless. On its roof the magpie, head cocked to the side, watched Mary stumble forward. *Crawk*, it called once as they approached.

"Hello!" Julee shouted. They slipped through the crack in the doors. "Hello?" she shouted again. The lights turned on.

"Oh hey," said Ben, surprised. He was lying on the cot near the wall. "You're here." He sat up straight and rubbed his eyes. Henry was sleeping in a chair, slumped over, with his head on the table next to the computer.

"Mary fell. I think she sprained her ankle, and she's scraped up pretty bad," said Julee.

"Oh..." Ben looked at Mary and winced, "oh... yeah... just a second, let me get my first-aid kit." He hopped off the cot and began digging through his backpack which lay beside him on the floor. "I have bandages and antiseptic and—"

"I broke the camera," said Mary suddenly, "when I fell. I landed on it. I'm sorry."

Ben froze and looked up. "Did you get the picture?"

"Yeah," Mary said, "but it's lost now."

"Not necessarily." It was Henry's voice. He had awoken and was staring, wide eyed, at Mary.

"What are you looking at," she snapped, "and what do you mean, not necessarily?"

Henry answered, still staring, his voice sounded almost... kind. "It's not necessarily lost. The picture should still be there, as long as the memory card isn't broken, let me see it." He took the camera from Elliot.

"Got it," said Ben, pulling two small white boxes from out of his backpack. He opened them and spoke to Julee. "Use the water purifier in the lake to clean off the wounds, and then spray them with this antiseptic." He held up a small white bottle. "There's all different sizes of bandages and gauze and tape you can use to cover up the worst of it."

Mary cringed at the words *the worst of it*. She wished she had a mirror so she could see what she looked like.

"The lens has been shattered," said Henry, "but the memory card is fine." He reached for a cord and plugged it into the camera and began typing on the computer keyboard.

"Come on Mary," said Julee, "follow us."

Mary followed Julee and Elliot out of the cave and down to the lake. Elliot used the water purifier to pump clean water onto the cuts in Mary's leg and arm and shoulder. To clean her face, Mary collected water in her cupped hands, and gently splashed it onto her cheek and forehead, which burned when she touched them. When the cuts were clean, Julee sprayed them with antiseptic—it felt cold—and taped large bandages onto Mary's knee and shoulder and some small bandages onto her cheek and forehead.

"Does it look bad?" Mary asked when Julee had finished.

"Not too bad," Julee answered, "makes you look tough." She winked and gently punched Mary's un-bandaged shoulder.

Mary smiled. "The picture!" She stood and limped as fast as she could back to the cave. Inside, Henry and Ben were sitting in front of the computer, staring at the screen. "What is it, what do you see?"

Ben wheeled around. "It's a galaxy, Mary. There's a whole galaxy. Look!"

There, next to the star of Andromeda's right knee, was a clear and perfect spiral of lights. An entire galaxy. Billions of stars. It had been hiding, too faint and distant to be seen without the Amazing Eye.

"What does it mean?" asked Elliot from behind. "Is it another clue?"

Mary stared. She blinked. She couldn't believe what she was seeing. It really was an entire galaxy. She had taken a real picture of a real galaxy. It had been right there in the sky, the whole time. It was the fuzzy spot she had seen two nights ago when she thought her eyes were just tired.

"Could it be... that simple?" Mary said. She took off her backpack, opened it, and pulled out the star-chart of the Andromeda constellation. She unfolded it carefully and lifted it up, allowing the fluorescent lights on the cave ceiling to shine through the paper from behind.

Something was there... something faint... something hiding... written in some nearly-invisible ink by Andromeda's right knee. It was a drawing of a spiral galaxy, and a map, and a series of twelve strange symbols...

CHAPTER 18

INTO THE DARK

"Mary, what is it?" asked Elliot.

"It's a map, and a combination... to unlock..." Mary pointed across the cavern, at the metal bars that seemed to belong in a jail and the black tunnel that led into the depths, where bats and glowing mice lived. She could almost feel the darkness seeping out of it. There was no moon-light or star-light, it was complete and total and utter darkness. "... to unlock *that* door."

Elliot gasped.

"Wow, let me see," said Ben. He stood behind Mary and gazed at the chart. "Yeah, it *is* a map... of the *tunnel*. See, there's the cave, and there's the tunnel entrance, where the metal bars are. There's a whole maze of tunnels down there."

"And here's an X," Mary pointed-out.

"like... *X marks the spot?*" asked Elliot.

Mary nodded. "Yeah. That's where it is. That's what I have to find."

"It's like a treasure map," said Ben, beaming. "Hey, I have a flashlight, in my backpack. I've been wanting to explore that tunnel since we first saw it."

Julee looked at him in disbelief. "Wait, you *want* to go in there?" she said.

"Sure," answered Ben, "why not?"

Julee shook her head slowly. "Well you can count me out."

"Yeah, me too," said Elliot quickly. "I don't want to go either."

Mary looked Ben in the eyes—they were twinkling. She didn't think it was possible to be so excited to enter a terrifyingly dark and scary tunnel, but his excitement gave her courage. "I guess it's just the two of us then," she said, and then glanced at Henry, "unless *you* want to go."

Henry looked nervous. "Why would *I* want to go in *there?*" He scoffed and crossed his arms, and then he quickly stood up and left the cave, through the crack in the massive doors, without saying another word.

Ben began rummaging through his backpack and pulled out a small flashlight. "It's ten LED's, so it's super bright." He turned the flashlight on—it *was* very bright, so bright that Mary had to shield her eyes when he pointed it at her.

"Oops, sorry," he said and turned the flashlight away. "Hey, can you walk alright?"

Mary nodded. "Yeah, I think so."

"Well." He swung his backpack over his shoulders. "Should we go?"

Mary nodded again. "Yeah, let's go." She zipped her backpack closed, put it on, and holding the star-chart map in hand, she limped to the back of the cave, towards the metal bars. She imagined, waiting in the tunnel, the glowing red eyes and flicking tongue of the serpent, the serpent from the myth, the serpent sent to devour the princess Andromeda. She imagined it eating her whole, her hands clawing at the cold stone floor as she slowly slipped down the serpent's throat. A wave of fear washed over her. The darkness of the tunnel was absolute. She took a deep breath. *I can do this. I can do this,* she thought to herself.

At the door, Ben held his flashlight behind the star-chart to illuminate the combination, while Mary spun the dial on the lock, one symbol after another, to match the sequence on the map. "These symbols look so familiar," said Mary. "I know I've seen them before." As soon as the twelfth and final symbol was entered, there was a soft click, and the metal bars swung open. The combination was correct.

Ben grinned with anticipation. "You ready?"

Mary took another deep breath. "Yeah." She remembered what Elliot had said, three days ago—was the door meant to keep something out, or keep something in? She hoped it was meant to keep something out. *What if there's something in there?* she thought, and was immediately glad that she hadn't said it out loud.

Ben directed the light inside—it lit the passage for a short distance before fading away into black. "The map showed this tunnel going down for a little ways, and then two tunnels branching off to the left, and then one to the right, and the X was in the second tunnel after that, on the right, after a couple of turns, in a long room."

Mary looked at Ben with surprise. "How do you remember all that?"

Ben shrugged. "I dunno, I'm good with maps I guess."

"Mary," said Elliot from behind, with her big, wide eyes and innocent smile. "Good luck."

Mary smiled back. "Thanks Elliot."

"Mary Andromeda, The *Un*-chained Princess," announced Julee, and winked. "Better you than me."

Mary winked back, and then suddenly, Ben grabbed Mary's hand. "Come on, let's get that treasure," he said. He held the flashlight with one hand, and Mary's hand with the other, and gently pulled her into the tunnel. Mary felt a sudden thrill of courage and excitement and then stepped with him, slowly, holding hands in the dark.

Ben pointed the flashlight up and down and left and right, scanning the walls and ceiling and floor of the tunnel as they walked forward. They turned a corner, and another, and

Mary looked behind her—the fluorescent lights of the cave were gone. The sound of the river in the valley was gone. She imagined the flashlight going out, and groping hopelessly in the dark, wandering deeper and deeper into the maze of tunnels, not knowing which way was out, lost forever in the absolute blackness and silence of the cave. "Are you sure that flashlight won't go off?" she asked uneasily.

"Yeah... pretty sure," said Ben. "If it does, I'd be able to get us out though. Hey, here's that first tunnel on the left." He aimed the flashlight into it—it looked exactly the same as the tunnel they were in. "I'll have to come back and explore that," he said excitedly.

They continued down, past the second tunnel on the left and one on the right. The slope of the tunnel was getting steeper. "I wonder where those bats live," said Ben, "they have to be down here somewhere. Hey wait a second. Mary, do you mind if I turn the light off, just for a minute. I think I see something up there."

Mary didn't want him to, but she was also curious. "Sure... okay... but just for a minute." Ben held her hand tighter and turned off the light. There was something glowing, just ahead, in a crack on the cave wall. They walked slowly towards it.

On the other side of the crack, which was just big enough to slip through, was a huge cavern; its ceiling was glowing. Long strands of greenish-blue glow-in-the-dark thread hung down from it, and glowing dots filled its cracks and crevices. It almost looked like the night sky.

"What is *that*?" marveled Ben.

Mary was speechless. How could it be? How could there be a glowing ceiling in the darkness of the cave? There was a chittering sound nearby and something scurried out of the crack. "Look, the mouse," said Mary. She watched it run along the wall of the tunnel and disappear around a corner.

"Glowing mice... glowing ceilings... this island is *crazy*," whispered Ben.

"Crazy *awesome*," added Mary, grasping Ben's had tighter. "Come on, let's get to that X."

Ben turned the flashlight back on, and they continued down the tunnel, eventually turning at the second right. Mary's ankle was hurting more with every step, but she tried not to notice it. Soon, she heard something that sounded like the hum of a motor, like when the observatory ceiling opened. The sound got louder and louder—as they seemed to be walking towards it—and before long, the tunnel ended and they emerged into a room and there was daylight coming in through a series of small windows high up on the wall.

Ben turned the flashlight off. The room was long and skinny, with a high ceiling, and it had a slight curve to it, like a bow or a crescent moon. The humming sound, along with the sound of rushing water, was coming from a large rectangular object in the middle of the room.

"Look, the walls are cement, not rock," Ben said. "I know where we are. We're inside the dam. That's the generator, that's what's making electricity for the observatory, and the lights in the cave." He let go of Mary's hand and ran forward, pointing at a bundle of pipes and wires that ran along the floor and into another tunnel at the opposite end of the room. "I bet that tunnel goes up to the House of Andromeda. These are access tunnels! I bet they connect everything. What if each tunnel goes to a different house? We could find them all!" He looked at Mary, beaming.

"Is this where the X is?" asked Mary. She glanced around. There were shelves filled with big wrenches and nuts and bolts along one wall, and a stack of pipes and coils of wire in the corner.

"Yeah, it was in *this* room," said Ben. "I know it."

They searched briefly and found nothing but motor parts and more tools and a control panel covered with switches and gauges. "Henry would *love* this," commented Ben.

Mary glanced up at the ceiling and down at the floor. In the middle of the room, set into the floor, were six squares, each about two feet wide, and not made of cement but made of stone. Each stone was carved with a different letter.

"Hey look at these," Mary said. There was a 'K' that had straight edges and looked like it was made out of rulers, there was a 'W' that looked like it was made out of mechanical arms, there was a 'K' with an extra line in the middle that made it look like a plus sign or a cross, there was a 'D' with circles behind it, there was a cursive 'W' that had leaves coming off of one end, and there was the spiral letter 'A' of the Andromeda House.

"I bet those are all the houses," said Mary, "of the Royal Fellowship Society. Each house has a different letter, just like mine."

"Hey, I think these stones lift up," exclaimed Ben. "See that thin crack around them, they're not attached to the floor, and there are small holes here." He crouched down and squeezed his fingers around the edges of the stone with the spiral letter 'A' and lifted. The stone moved. He pulled hard and brought the stone up, out of the floor, and slid it off to the side with a grunt. Underneath the stone was a black box.

"X marks the spot," said Ben.

Mary pulled out the box easily and sat on the floor and opened it. On top of some papers and journals were two computer memory sticks, a video disc, two cassette tapes, and a small plastic case that had wires sticking out of it. "We'd need the computer for these," Mary said and set them carefully aside. She pulled out the top sheet of paper. It was a note, from her grandfather to her mother, written in the same scribbled handwriting as the riddle from the book about nebulae.

Dearest Vera,

The truth will set you free.

Use it wisely.

Your loving father,

Galileo Andromeda

"The truth will set you free," said Ben, nodding. "I like that."

"It's for my mom," said Mary, puzzled. "My grandpa hid this for my mom, not for me." She set the note aside.

"Look, the next one's about an explosion," said Ben. Mary pulled out the paper—it was a newspaper article. The gray newsprint was damp from the moisture in the dam. It was dated eight years ago, when Mary was three years old.

She read it aloud:

Tragic Explosion Kills 6 Scientists

The deaths of six scientists, members of the preeminent community of scientific nobility, The Royal Fellowship Society, shocked the world yesterday. Astronomer sisters Cecilia and Anne Andromeda (of the famous Andromeda Family), Albert and James Kelvin (sons of the mathematician and engineer Archimedes Kelvin), J.J. Dalton (oldest son of chemists Democritus and Marie Dalton), and Richard Ki (renowned biologist and author), were pronounced dead Monday from an explosion that occurred at an undisclosed location The direct cause of the explosion is unknown but is reported to have been accidental.

"Our community of science will never be the same," commented Alfred Watt, engineer, businessman, and co-founder (with Isaac Kelvin) of the Institute, an elite science and technology school in Port Oceanside. "This immeasurable loss of genius is a severe blow to scientific research. It is a tragic, tragic loss. The discoveries of these six great minds will be remembered forever as some of the greatest and most profound in all of science."

Albert Kelvin, perhaps the most notable of those deceased, and the youngest of the great Kelvin brothers, is well known for transforming the fields of Physics and Astronomy with his revolutionary theories concerning space, time, and the power of the imagination. He is survived by his mother, Emmy Euler; older brothers Isaac and Michael; wife, Vera Andromeda; and two young daughters, Maria Estelle and Cassiopeia Nova Andromeda. He was 29 years old.

"Wow," whispered Ben, "sounds like your dad was awesome. Only 29 years old and he did all that?"

"Yeah... it sounds like they *all* were. *Some of the greatest discoveries in all of science,* it says."

"... and *the famous Andromeda family,*" Ben added, in an impressed voice. "Hey, isn't that Henry's last name—Kelvin?"

"Yeah," answered Mary, "Elliot said his family started the Institute. His father must be Isaac Kelvin, my dad's older brother."

Ben thought for moment. "But that would mean you two are—"

"Cousins," said Mary. "I know."

"Wow," exclaimed Ben, "I did not see *that* coming. You and Henry are *cousins?*"

"Yeah, I think so," Mary continued, "and look at this name, Richard Ki, that's Elliot's last name, remember, she said it sounds like the word key but it's spelled K-i. Maybe they're related. Maybe Elliot's here for a reason too. And it says here the explosion was an accident, and that it occurred at an *undisclosed location*. That has to be Evergreen Isle, remember how the RFS promised to keep it a secret? I haven't seen anything that looks... exploded, have you?"

Ben looked at Mary curiously. "Wait, so you and Henry are *cousins*? Your dad and Henry's dad are brothers? You have the same grandparents?"

Mary pushed her glasses farther up her nose. "Yeah," she shrugged. She imagined shaking hands with Henry after a pretend sword-fight, in a friendly truce. She looked back in the box and pulled out a stack of photographs. "Here, shine the light over there, I can't see from the glare."

Ben adjusted the light so that the photographs were visible and Mary flipped through them. "They look like... photographs of the cave," she said, "before it was all destroyed. See, here are those long tables, and the bookshelves, and the cages, and there's the tunnel in the background."

"I wonder what all that equipment was for," said Ben, "and where it went... there's tons of it." The photos showed the cave filled with computers and glass beakers and machines.

Behind the pictures of the cave was one other photograph that was different. It was on older-looking paper, and it was of five boys, standing on the dam, wearing shorts. They looked like they had just gone swimming. The lake was behind them, and the massive cave doors were in the background, to the right. They were young, around Ben's age or a little older, and they were smiling and had their arms over each other's shoulders. Mary turned the picture over. It was labeled in Galileo Andromeda's scribbled hand-writing:

Alfred Watt and the Kelvin brothers: Isaac, Michael, James, and Albert. Upon completion of the Kelvin and Watt Dam and Laboratory.

"Your dad lived here too?" asked Ben.

Mary flipped the picture back over and looked at the boys. "They *all* lived here. They grew up here, just like my mom."

"Maybe the tower was *his* house," said Ben. "The Kelvin House?"

"Or this other boy's, Alfred Watt," said Mary. "He's the same one from the article, that started the Institute with Henry's dad."

Mary placed the photographs aside and pulled from the box a packet of blue-lined graph paper.

"Those look like blue-prints," said Ben.

Mary flipped through them. They were covered in drawings and equations. Some of the drawings looked like plans for rockets or buildings, and some of them looked like maps, but Mary couldn't tell for sure. She set the blueprints aside and pulled out the last object, a journal. *"The Journal of Isaac Kelvin and Alfred Watt,"* she read. She flipped through it. "It has something to do with... weapons... and..." Mary gasped, "...explosives." She looked up at Ben. "Maybe *they* caused it, Alfred and Isaac, this must be the evidence that proves it. They're the ones my mom needed to expose."

Ben looked puzzled. "Henry's dad caused the explosion that killed your father, and your aunts, and all those scientists? But Isaac Kelvin was your dad's brother, why would he—"

"Shhh," Mary said, "did you hear that?" She cocked her ear towards the tunnel entrance. The sound of the generator and rushing water were loud behind her but there was a faint voice, echoing down through the tunnel, from far above.

"Mary... Help..."

Mary knew that voice. It wasn't Julee, or Elliot, or Henry. It was her sister's voice. It was Cassie!

"Mary... Help..."

"That's my sister!" She quickly refilled the box, stood, and took off towards the voice, limping and clutching the black box under her arm.

"Mary... Help..."

"What is Cassie doing here? This doesn't make sense." Mary entered the tunnel. "Ouch!" Her left ankle twisted and a sharp throbbing pain shot up her leg. She took another step and stumbled and leaned up against the cold, wet rock.

"Here, let me help you," said Ben. He took the box and put Mary's left arm around his shoulder and gave her the flashlight. "Put as little weight on it as you can."

"Mary... Help..." Cassie's voice was getting louder.

"Come on!" Mary said, frantically. They hobbled up the tunnel together. "I don't understand. This doesn't make sense. Why would Cassie be here?" They turned a corner... and another... and were back in the main passage.

"Mary... Help..."

Mary limped faster. She imagined the serpent behind her, slithering closer in the dark as she limped in slow motion, its mouth open, its fangs unsheathed, ready to strike, but she couldn't move fast enough.

"Mary... Help..."

As they turned the last corner, Mary saw the fluorescent lights of the cave at the end of the long tunnel. A figure was silhouetted there, backlit from the light behind.

"Mary!" shouted Cassie, and then another figure pulled her away, out of sight.

Mary let go of Ben and hopped forward, on one foot, as fast as she could go—up, up out of the tunnel. She burst into the open cavern and collapsed, exhausted, on all fours. Cassie was standing there, in the middle of the room, a terrified look in her eyes. Elliot and Julee were cowering against the wall. And Henry was sitting at the computer table, arms crossed, with a satisfied look on his face.

"What's this?" said a calm, cold, heartless voice from the corner.

CHAPTER 19

THE UNION OF POWER

It was Uncle Edwin, in his gray suit and silver tie, grinning smugly.

"Mary, I'm sorry," Cassie said, fighting back tears. "He made me call for you. I—"

"Silence girl," spoke Edwin calmly. He turned to the black box in Ben's hands. "Bring that to me, boy."

Ben gulped and looked at Mary, as if he was asking for her permission. Mary nodded, and Ben walked across the room and gave the box to Uncle Edwin and then returned to Mary's side. Uncle Edwin opened it, sifted through its contents, and then chuckled and smiled wickedly. "Well done

Mary," he said. He fixed his eyes upon her. She couldn't stand—her ankle hurt too badly. She sat on the cold stone floor, motionless, as if she were chained there. "I'm impressed... we've been searching for this box for years. Perhaps you're more like your parents than I gave you credit for. But then again, I knew you would serve a purpose someday."

"Where's my mother?" said Mary angrily, "and my grandmother? Where are they? Tell me!"

Uncle Edwin merely laughed. "Girl, your mother hasn't been seen in six years. She left you and disappeared. And your grandmother died before you were born." Uncle Edwin grinned and seemed to relish in the puzzled and defeated look on Mary's face. "Oh, I knew about your little fantasy—your pretend Grandmother Caroline. How convenient for me that an elderly stranger worked in a bookshop named Caroline's Corner, and that you found a journal with your grandmother's hand-writing. You should never have opened that door, Mary." He laughed again. "Oh I knew you couldn't resist believing that *she* was behind it all, that it was all for *you*, that you were *meant* to be here, to learn *the truth*. Ha. Silly girl. You have quite the imagination, don't you Mary?   We knew your grandfather hid this for your mother, he told us before he died. We just needed someone from the *famous Andromeda family* to track it down for us. To *follow the clues*." He chuckled. "Clever little girl you are. Now the Union of Power is unstoppable. Now we can—"

"Edwin—" came a voice from outside, a man's voice that was deep and rich and not at all unpleasant. Its speaker was just out of sight, just behind the massive doors. "Do you have the box... or not?"

Edwin continued to stare at Mary. "Yes, I have it."

"Is the picture there... and the plans?" he asked.

"Yes," Edwin replied.

"Then it's time to leave."

Edwin glanced at Cassie and then back at Mary and frowned, as if he were pretending to be sad, and said in a calm, sarcastic voice, "Goodbye Maria. Goodbye Cassiopeia. The last six years have been... unfortunate."

"Wait," said Cassie, puzzled, "you're just going to leave us here?"

"Well I'm certainly not going to *kill* you, and you're certainly not coming back with me, so yes, I'm just going to leave you here."

"But—" Cassie began, and then saw the expression on Mary's face. The expression of total defeat. The expression of utter hopelessness. The expression of a beautiful princess, shackled to a rock, and left for dead by everyone that should have loved her. Mary's head hung down, and her glasses slipped off her nose and fell to the floor. She didn't bother to pick them up, she just sat there, hunched over, staring vacantly at the ground.

As Edwin walked towards the door, Henry stood and followed behind. "Goodbye new-kids," he scoffed. "It's been... unfortunate." Edwin slipped out of the cave, and Henry followed, and the deep voice spoke again.

"What are *you* doing, Boy?"

"I'm coming with you, Father," answered Henry. "You're not going to leave me here, are you?"

"Did *you* open the door, or was it the girl?" asked the voice.

"It was the girl, Father," answered Henry.

"So did you succeed, or did you fail?"

"I helped her… and I doubted her… just like you told me… to make her angry… so that she would *want* to prove me wrong. It was easy. She played right into it, just like you said. We got the box didn't we?"

"We…?" Isaac Kelvin laughed. "What did you do that was *your* idea, that didn't come from *me* first? What are you worth Henry? Do you have original thoughts… original plans? You build robotic luggage, and tinker with things that other, much greater minds have made. When I was your age…"

There was a long pause, and Mary heard footsteps on the gravel outside.

"But Father—"

The footsteps stopped. "Give me your phone, boy. If you can get off this island alive, then perhaps you will be worthy… worthy of your family name."

The footsteps continued again and were soon followed by the tremendous roar of an engine which quickly trailed away into the sky.

"Mary!" shouted Cassie as she ran to her sister, "are you okay? What happened to you?" She knelt down and threw her arms around Mary's neck. Something about Cassie's voice, and her touch, and her smell, made Mary burst into tears.

"Oh Cassie." Mary cried... and cried... and Cassie cried too. Tears streamed down Mary's face and she sobbed, cradled in Cassiopeia's arms, for a long time. "Oh Cassie, I missed you." She sat upright and wiped her eyes with the back of her hand.

"Mary, your eyes are so pretty," Cassie said, smiling. She picked Mary's glasses off the floor and gently put them over Mary's ears, and Mary pushed them farther up her nose.

"I'm sorry Cassie, I don't know where Mom is, I don't know anything. It's all my fault."

"It's not your fault, Mary. Here, let me help you up." Cassie grabbed Mary under the arm and helped her stand. "What happened to you anyway?"

"Oh... I tripped... and fell... again." Mary limped towards the chairs at the computer table. Ben was standing there, with Julee and Elliot.

"Mary!" they shouted together, and hugged her, and Julee helped her sit down.

"Ben told us about the dam, and the hidden box, and the explosion, and Henry's father," said Elliot.

"Did he tell you we were cousins?" asked Mary.

Elliot's jaw dropped and Julee shook her head slowly.

"Henry's father is my uncle." She glanced at Cassie. "*Our* uncle. Our dad's last name was Kelvin. He was the youngest of four brothers. They grew up here too, like Mom."

"Mom grew up here?" asked Cassie, puzzled.

Mary nodded and grabbed Cassie's hand—she had so much to tell her. "Hey everyone, this is my little sister, Cassie. Cassie, this is Elliot, Julee, and Ben." Mary pointed out each of them, and while they were all shaking hands and greeting each other, something caught Mary's eye in the doorway. It was Henry, peeking in through the crack in the massive doors. She was angry at him... but she wasn't... she didn't know how she felt. "You called him, didn't you?" she shouted across the room. "Your phone worked this whole time, you were just waiting for me to open those bars. You knew this whole time."

Henry slowly stepped in, his head hung down. He slumped back against the wall of the cave, next to the door. He didn't reply, he just stared at the ground.

"Your father caused it," said Mary, bitterly. "Your father caused the accident. It was an explosion, and it killed my dad, and my mom's sisters. And it was your father that caused it and—"

"We're cousins?" interrupted Henry.

Mary looked away. "Yes."

"The great Albert Kelvin was your father?"

Mary looked back at Henry. His eyes were wide open, like he was impressed.

"Yes."

"I know everything about him. I've read all his papers. He's one of the greatest scientists that... you think my father caused his death? He's not dead, he only disappeared, eight years ago."

"No," Mary argued, "he died in an explosion, here on Evergreen Isle, we saw the newspaper article. Your dad and someone else, Alfred Watt, were making explosives, and they caused it. That's what was in that box, Henry, evidence. Evidence against them, evidence that proved they did it."

"I don't believe you. President Watt and my father would not have *killed* Albert Kelvin. You're jumping to conclusions."

Mary scowled. "*President* Watt is it? Maybe that's just what they want you to believe at the *Institute*."

"Your father could be alive," continued Henry. "No one ever saw his body. Believe me, there is no evidence that he is dead for certain."

"What is this, just doubting me so that I want to prove you wrong? I don't care what you think, Henry. You can stay down here and—arrrrr!" She grabbed a piece of paper from the desk, crumpled it up, and threw it at him. It fell short. "Come on, Cassie," she said and struggled out of the chair. Julee helped her stand, and Mary put her arm around Julee's shoulders and limped towards the door. Cassie and Elliot followed.

"Mary..." said Ben. "Um... I'm gonna stay down here... I'll come up to the house later."

Mary spun around. "Oh don't you feel sorry for him," she snapped. "He doesn't deserve it."

Ben looked away, and Mary hobbled out of the cave, out into the fresh air of the island, where they were now stranded for certain, where there was a blue sky, and a gentle breeze, and light from the glorious sun shining down upon them.

CHAPTER 20

THE FIRST JOURNAL

As Mary slowly limped back up the hill, with Julee, Elliot, and Cassie beside her, Cassie told them her story:

She had been locked in her room for the past four days, ever since Mary had been sent away, when just an hour ago, Uncle Edwin had burst in and dragged her by the hand to the back lawn, where there was some kind of rocket-plane, a kind she had never seen before, waiting for them. Along with Uncle Edwin, and the man they now knew was Isaac Kelvin, Henry's father, there were two other passengers, a man and a women, both with straight black hair, that didn't speak and that looked nervous.

The rocket-plane took off and flew for no more than ten minutes, Cassie thought, at an incredible speed, before landing just outside the cave doors, beside the stone tower. Uncle Edwin and Isaac Kelvin got out and pushed Cassie into the cave and Julee and Elliot were made to sit against the wall, and Cassie was made to call for help.

"So, what is this place?" asked Cassie. "And why are you here? And why aren't you at the Institute? And Mom grew up here? And that boy is our cousin? And what about that other boy, what was his name again, the one with the blond hair? And what's that journal that Uncle Edwin was talking about, from Caroline's Corner? And what was in that box? And is anyone else here? And... where are we going?"

Mary smiled. It felt so good to hear Cassie's voice— her innocent curiosity and her cheerful spirit. As she was listening to the barrage of questions, Mary realized something —she realized how calm she felt, now that she and Cassie were together again, despite what had just happened, despite her uncle setting up the whole thing, despite being tricked into finding the box.

"We're going home, Cassie," Mary answered. "We're going home." And she told her sister everything, with Julee and Elliot's help, as they walked slowly through the ancient forest, and collected apples in the orchard, and stood in the sundial—it was two in the afternoon—and stared up at the towering snow-capped peak which was ever guarding over them.

They all gave Cassie a tour of the Andromeda house, and Mary told Elliot about the man from the accident, Richard

Ki, but Elliot didn't recognize the name. At one point, Elliot looked nervous and asked, "Mary, how are we going to get home now? I miss my parents," but there was a hint of doubt in her voice, as if part of her didn't *want* to leave, and before Mary had a chance to reply, Elliot had been distracted by more of Cassie's questions.

In fact, as night approached, while they stood in the kitchen looking at the small pile of food that remained, Mary was surprised herself at how unconcerned she was of their situation: stranded, for certain, with seemingly no hope of rescue or a way off the island.

She imagined her Grandmother Caroline, cooking something on the stove, and her mother, cutting vegetables from the garden, and her Aunt Annie, washing the dishes, and her Aunt Cecelia, sweeping the floor. She imagined her mother looking out the window and seeing Mary's father, Albert Kelvin, running up the path to visit her. She remembered the document about the Royal Fellowship Society, how the founders agreed to keep the estates secret and self-sufficient.

Soon, Julee had made a stack of peanut-butter crackers which she carried to the couches in the great room, and they all ate together. There were so many unanswered questions, Mary thought, like: *were* there four more houses on the island, and where *was* the explosion, and what is the Union of Power doing anyway? She even wondered, to her surprise, who, if anyone, was really dead? She thought about what Henry had said, about no one ever seeing her dad's body. Maybe he was right. She knew that she couldn't believe anything her Uncle Edwin had ever said, and if a journal from her grandmother could be fake, then a newspaper article about the accident could be fake too, or maybe incorrect.

She didn't know what to believe. She felt like she was hardly closer to solving the mystery of her mother's departure, or the accident, then she was four days ago. She needed to know more. She needed to explore. *It's time you learned the truth*, she thought. And then she realized that the truth was, that she didn't know *what* the truth was, but that was okay, somehow. She remembered the look in Ben's eyes when he wanted to explore the island, to search for other houses, as if the mystery was the most exciting thing in the world.

"What is it Mary?" said Cassie. "What are you thinking about? You have that look that you get sometimes."

"Oh, I was just thinking about something in the box," Mary said, "a letter, from our grandpa to Mom. It said *the truth will set you free*. I was thinking, I don't know the truth... about where Mom is, about what really happened on this island... not yet... but I feel free here, much more than I ever felt at Uncle Edwin's, and I'm *glad* he left us. I'm *glad* I'm here, with you all, on Evergreen Isle."

"You're un-chained, girl, I'm tellin' you," said Julee. "It started when you came out of that observatory, on the first night. You had a look in your eyes like... like you *found* something... something... free-ing. It's the same look that Wild gets sometimes."

"Yeah, you really did." Elliot nodded. "You get that look every time you go in there."

Mary smiled and took a deep breath. She knew it also. "I wish I hadn't broken the camera though," she sighed.

"There has to be *hundreds* of objects up there... hiding... like the Andromeda galaxy. I want to see them *all*. I want to learn *everything* about them." Mary remembered the piles of journals in the Forbidden Room: journals about Evergreen Isle, journals by her mom and her aunts and her grandma. She remembered the journal from Caroline's Corner. It was still sitting in her violin case by the front door of the house. "Hold on a second, there's something I have to do." She hopped on one foot to the front door and hopped back to the couches, holding the case.

"Hey, it's your violin," exclaimed Cassie. "Oh, I wish I had mine."

Mary opened the side pocket and pulled out the journal.

"Is that the one that Uncle Edwin planted? The one you thought was from grandma?" asked Cassie.

"Yeah," Mary said and opened it to the first page. *"Mary, it's time you learned the truth. Follow the clues. Caroline,"* she read aloud. "Ya know, I kind of like that, even though it wasn't grandma who wrote it." She shrugged. "Because I *am* going to learn the truth... about everything... about the whole universe... and I think grandma would like that."

"Girl, you *know* she would," said Julee.

Mary smiled from ear to ear. She reached over the side of the couch and picked up a pen from the side table and uncapped it. "And, I think I'll keep the note there for another reason... to remind me," said Mary.

"To remind you of what?" asked Elliot.

"Not to get fooled again," grinned Mary. In her mind flashed the image of a lioness, roaming freely through her uncle's mansion and through dark tunnels and on beaches and over grass-covered hills and inside the observatory. Her observatory. She looked down at the journal and wrote, just below the forged message from her uncle:

The Journal of Mary Andromeda

"Ya know, we have all these rooms, and beds," Mary said as she closed the journal and set it on the side table. "We could each have a bedroom ya know."

The others thought for a moment.

"I kinda like sleeping here," said Elliot.

"Yeah, me too," said Julee. "It makes this whole place less... creepy at night."

"This place isn't creepy," said Mary. "We've cleaned it all up. There's just that broken window in my Aunt Annie's turret, and... well... I guess there are still those bugs in the flour." And she followed with a mysterious, "ooohhhhh," sound.

"Girl, don't bring *up* stuff like that," said Julee, with her fist raised, like when she would punch Ben in the shoulder. "That *Wild* boy is a bad influence." She stared at Mary seriously, and Mary stared back, and then they both burst into laughter.

That night, the girls stayed up late, talking and laughing and wondering, about what to do next, and where to explore, and what to do about Henry. They decided that if Henry's father would leave him here, there must be a way off the island, somehow, they just needed to figure it out. This thought reassured Elliot especially.

Mary showed Cassie the telescope and together they stared into the night sky for hours, and Cassie was, naturally, amazed. When they finally agreed to go to sleep, and were lying on the couches, tucked under the covers, waiting in silence, Elliot spoke:

"Hey, have you guys been imagining things lately. I feel like, ever since we got here I've been imagining all these things, just like, little scenes flashing in my mind. Is that weird?"

"Yeah, me too," agreed Julee, "and I've been havin' some funky dreams the past few nights."

Mary smiled to herself. She listened to the ocean surf, and the gentle notes of the wind-chimes, and the sound of her heartbeat, and of her friends' breathing, and slowly, she slipped into a dream...

✧ ✧ ✧

She was lying on her back and floating through the heavens. Countless stars spun around her and passed through her—glowing specks of dust, billions of them, dancing weightless in space. She looked at her wrists and there were chains around them, but she didn't care. She pulled against them gently, and they dissolved away—in a puff of wind—and became stars themselves. She looked in her hand and saw that she was holding a tiny serpent, no bigger than her palm. She inspected it closely, and smiled, and then softly brushed it away, into the beautiful night.

THE BOY GENIUS

"Hey Henry, do you really think Mary's dad could be alive," asked Ben. He was sitting in the cave, at the long computer table, with a pencil in hand, and he was drawing a map.

"Albert Kelvin is my hero," said Henry from the corner. He was lying on his cot and staring up at the ceiling. "I've wanted to find him since... as long as I can remember... and an old newspaper article proves nothing."

Ben continued to draw. The two boys listened to the drip-drip-dripping sound that came from somewhere in the cave. It was dusk outside. The bats would fly through the cavern soon, in their nightly migration from the tunnel, to catch and eat bugs out in the open air, out on the moonlit island.

beep beep

Ben jumped. "What was that?" he said, startled.

Henry sat upright and looked around, trying to locate the sound. *beep beep* "It's coming from over there, by your things!"

Ben dropped his pencil and hurried to his cot, where he had left his backpack and vest.

beep beep

He put his ear down and listened. *beep beep* "It's coming from my vest." He lifted it up and held it in front of him. *beep beep* He dug around in one pocket, and then another, and then another. "I don't know what it is," he said. "It's not in a pocket."

beep beep

"Here, let me see," said Henry. He took the vest from Ben's hands. *beep beep* "I think it's been sewn into the fabric. See, look at these extra stitches, and there's something in there, you can feel it."

beep beep

Ben unzipped a pocket on his backpack and pulled out a small pocket knife. *beep beep* He carefully cut into the vest, around the extra stitches, and removed a small black object.

beep beep

"I know what *that* is," exclaimed Henry, "it's a wireless receiver." Ben gave him the object and Henry carried it briskly to the computer. *beep beep* "It should work, even with this old computer. It can't send messages, but it must have received one."

Ben looked puzzled. *beep beep* "Why would that be sewn into my vest? My mom said it was my dad's old vest."

Henry plugged the receiver into the computer. The beeping stopped, a tiny green light turned on, and a message appeared on the computer screen...

We know where you are — the RFS

coming soon…

HENRY KELVIN

AND THE

MARVELOUS MOTOR

visit storiesinscience.com for news and updates

More to Explore

The story you have just read contains references to people and events in science history, and to technologies of the present and future. It is the author's opinion that the best way to learn about something is to research it for yourself — to follow your own curiosity. The following short list may be helpful in choosing a topic for a school project, or simply as search terms for further exploration.

Scientists you might find interesting

Caroline Herschel	Vera Rubin
Edwin Hubble	Albert Einstein
Annie Jump Cannon	Cecelia Payne
Galileo Galilei	

Emerging and advanced technologies

Autonomous cars	Delivery drones

Genetic engineering (cloning and gene editing)

Important events in science history

Galileo Galilei's *The Starry Messenger*

The Royal Society

For additional educational information related to *The Journals of Evergreen Isle* series, visit: storiesinscience.com

ABOUT THE AUTHOR

 Before beginning *The Journals of Evergreen Isle* book series, author J.G. Kemp taught high school Earth and space science, biology, and physics, and earned degrees in both educational curriculum and instruction, and visual and performing arts. He lives in Colorado Springs, Colorado, with his family, abundant sunshine, a large backyard garden, and the great mountains ever calling him home.

For news, updates, and **additional clues** to the mystery of Evergreen Isle and the Royal Fellowship Society, follow him online at: www.facebook.com/storiesinscience

CPSIA information can be obtained
at www.ICGtesting.com
Printed in the USA
FSHW04n1949190418
47231FS